Understanding Swift: for C and C++ Programmers while having to learn as little Object-C as possible

by David Francis Curran

Bullray cover photograph © 2016 Ian Scott/Adobe Stock

This book is dedicated to Wild-Wild-E (Wiley) July 4, 1997 to Jan 12, 2016

Understanding Swift for C and C++ programmers while having to learn as little Object-C as possible

by David Francis Curran

This book is intended for people who have some background in C and C++. It is not really intended for complete beginners to programming. If you'd like to understand Swift I strongly urge you to learn about C and/or C++ or another before tackling Swift.

I had to learn Object-C to port my programs from C and C++ to work on Macs and iPads. Swift gives you a chance to skip Object-C in a large part. This series of books was written to help you bridge the gap without having to spend a great deal of time learning Object-C. In later parts we will discuss how to include C or C++ into a Swift project. That inclusion will involve some Object-C. But I hope to enable you to write code in Swift such that you may decide to use Swift rather than C or C++.

Many years ago I believed I had a problem understanding math. Apparently many imaginative people do. I had let the idea of math overwhelm me. Then one very good teacher teaching a calculus class I took over the summer started the class by explaining that he was going to tell us everything there was to know about math in the known universe. He said: One plus one is two: that's addition.

Understanding Swift

Two minus one is one: that's subtraction.

Two times two is four: that's multiplication.

Four divided by two is two: that's division.

And that is all there is. The complicated part of math we learned in grade school. Every math formula can be broken down to combinations of these four simple parts.

I do not know how much you know or remember about programming C or C++, or what you know about Swift already. Because I don't know what you know I will be explaining the simple parts.

This book is intended as programmed instruction. I am going to try and program your brain to master the subject of the Swift Language. It is intended that you answer all the quiz questions at the end of each section. I have hidden some tidbits there that by solving will increase your knowledge. For example, Question 7 in the Constants and Variables section has a casting method we did not cover in the text. Just because a subject isn't covered doesn't mean it won't work. How to find such things in the xCode references is explained too. Don't worry about mistakes when evaluating things in your playground. (Although you do need to remove them or comment them out before continuing. An error will halt the playground's ability evaluate what you've entered.) Keep in mind the best programmers are the one who have made the most mistakes and learned by them.

Note: This work Understanding Swift for C and C++ programers is being published in sections for two reasons.

1) To try and keep up with changes in Swift.

2) To allow as many images as possible without having to limit them due to size of file size limitations (on uploads) on Kindle.

I hope you enjoy this book as much as I did putting it together.

The code for projects in this book is available online at http://geniusat.work/swift.php. For the code for playgrounds simply copy the code off the page and paste it into your playground. The reason individual playground code is not online is we will be changing the code so often, i.e. changing single lines in playgrounds to emphasis errors, that including all possible playground code would be unwieldy and confusing.

Understanding Swift

one

Download The Program

Understanding Swift

To run swift on your Mac you'll need to download the latest version. Operating system requirements — (i.e. What version of the Mac OS X you'll need to run the latest version of Xcode) will be explained there. Xcode is FREE. You only need to pay to become a Mac developer. But if you are just learning to program or just coming from C or C++ to Swift you won't need to worry about that just yet.

Note that there may be new beta versions available. Here for example (Figure 1.1) there is a 6.4 beta 2 which offers programming for the Apple Watch. For now, I'd stick with the current version. So download and come back when you've got Xcode running.

Figure 1.1 Apple's Xcode download page

Understanding Swift

two

Lets Start Programming

Understanding Swift

Don't worry if you dare unfamiliar with any of the terms below. You'll learn more about what they are as we go on.

With Swift you can set up a "executable program" or you can set up a "playground." You can set up a "Cocoa application" or a "command line application." And you can even run Swift in your "terminal."

* A Cocoa application is an application that runs in a window with buttons and text fields and your code operates depending on what input you enter. And your results show up in a graphical interface. (Figure 2.1)

You solution will appear here. If the solve takes more than 60 seconds or has more than 30000 characters (i.e. there are heck of a lot of solutions) the app will terminate.

Note That if you hit solve with the CR#SSWXRD CRYPTXGRAM crosswXrd cryptXgram text in place as is (both lower and upper case) the solution will appear after a time. HOWEVER if you push the uppercase button and covert the CR#SSWXRD CRYPTXGRAM crosswXrd cryptXgram to all upper case the solve will fail. CROSSWXRD will be identified as a misspelling since O can't be represented by both a CAPITAL O and a CAPITAL X. Try replacing the CR#SSWXRD CRYPTXGRAM crosswXrd cryptXgram text with our quote from Hamlet below. (If a cryptogram is not in uppercase covert to uppercase and then solve.)

GL YV LI MLG GL YV GSZG RH GSV JFVHGRLM DSVGSVI RG RH MLYOVI RM GSV NRMW GL HFUUVI GSV HORMTH ZMW ZIILDH LU LFGIZTVLFH ULIGFMV ZMW YB LKKLHRMT VMW GSVN. LI GL WIVZN GL WIVZM KVIXSZMXV GL HOVVK

By the way the above quote from Hamlet should fill the text box and that is about the max of words you can solve for at the one time. The box will scroll but DO NOT OVER FILL.

If you need more solving power or want more bells and whistles the Mac OSX version has a lot more fire power and settings. Note That dictionary size affects speed. Although some puzzles require larger dictionaries -- some puzzles will have too many solutions with bigger dictionaries.

For a link to a video tutorial for solving crosswords, cryptograms, and hangman puzzles at http://geniusAt.work

You must enter text below. Cryptograms in ALL CAPS .
Hit solve & your results will appear in the text box above.

| Small Dictionary | Medium Dictionary | Large Dictionary |

CR#SSWXRD CRYPTXGRAM crosswXrd cryptXgram

Understanding Swift

 * A command line application, which is what we will be demonstrating soon, is an application where you enter text and see your output as text rather than in graphics.

* With an executable command line application, you hit run when you are done programming and if you don't need to debug it, (i.e. There are no errors in your code.) it will execute. (Figure 2.2) And your results will appear in the Debug Areas Output window. (Figure 2.3)

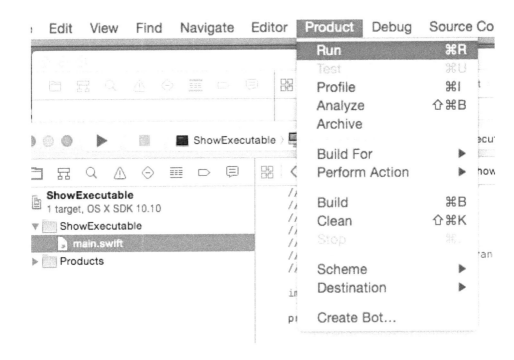

Figure 2.2 Run executes an executable file.

Understanding Swift

* With a Swift playground you write code and see the immediate result of that code in an area called the gutter. It is a great way to test your Swift code. Lets set a playground up right now and we can begin testing code. (We will cover running swift in your terminal a little later.)

Open Xcode and under FILE select New and then Playground. (Figure 2.4)

Figure 2.4 Open a new playground with File -> New -> Playground.

You can name your playground anything you like. I've named mine
myUnderstandingSwiftPlayground. (Figure 2.5) Note that I've set my platform to the default
OS X. For now set yours to OS X.

Choose options for your new file:

Name   MyUnderstandingSwiftPlayground

Platform: OS X

Cancel   Previous   Next

Figure 2.5 MyUnderstandingSwiftPlayground. USING OS X

When you hit next your playground will open. To the left below is the code section where you enter your code. To the right is the gutter which shows immediate feedback on your code. (Figure 2.6) Here the gutter simply repeats your string.

Understanding Swift

You are all set to start learning code.

Chapter Questions

1) A Cocoa application has a

A. Text based interface.

B. Graphical interface.

C. funny interface.

B. both a text and graphical interface.

2) An executable program

A. Is no different than a playground.

B. Is Superior to a playground.

C. Executes when you RUN it.

D. Runs itself.

3) An executable program prints it's results

A. On the internet.

B. In the playground.

C. In the Debug Area's Output window.

D. On television.

4) Feedback on entries to a playground appear in

A. In the Debug Area's Output window.

B. The gutter.

C. The internet.

D. A graphical Interface.

Understanding Swift

Understanding Swift

A few introductory notes.

You may download playgrounds and projects with either:

http://www.geniusat.work/SwiftForC_CplusplusCode.sitx

or

http://www.geniusat.work/SwiftForC_CplusplusCode.zip

The playgrounds or projects chapters contain the text you may paste into Swift. Just delete any author notes that may be attached by your chosen reader.

Comment inclusion is pretty much as it is in C and C++. I am mentioning it first as you may need to comment out errors you'll make as we go along.

As I said in the foreword: The best programmer is the one whose made the most mistakes and learned by them.

```
// makes a line a comment
/* makes a longer comment over many lines */
```

They are both not included in a program or a playground as code.

The two declarations below introduced by var are like

```
        int bananas = 5;
                and
        int grapes = 6;
```

in C and C++ though they are more than ints. We will talk more about this in Constants and Variables. But for now this is simply an example for printing.

var **bananas** = 5 // note this used to not have the () at the end but that has been changed.

var **grapes** = 6

/* note this used to not have the ()

at the end but that has been changed. */

Print has replaced println

When Swift came out println( ) was the way to print to the something. Apple has changed this to print(). But think of it still as println because it prints a line including a return \n at the end. You will see this in action soon. To print a variable or constant within a print() statement you would use something like print("We have \(grapes)" grapes and \(bananas) bananas").

print("We have \(grapes) grapes and \(bananas) bananas")

Note QUOTES MUST NOT BE SMART QUOTES.

Swift's default for the end of a print() is \n, however we can by change that if we wish with the terminator: extension. Type this into a playground:

print("We have \(apples) apples and \(oranges) oranges", terminator: "")
print(" and \(pears) pears")

```
print("We have \(grapes) grapes and \(bananas) bananas")   "We have 6 gr:

var apples = 4                                              4
var oranges = 5                                             5

var pears = 6                                               6

print("We have \(apples) apples and \(oranges) oranges",   "We have 4 ap
    terminator: "")
print(" and \(pears) pears")                               " and 6 pears\
```

```
We have 6 grapes and 5 bananas
We have 4 apples and 5 oranges and 6 pears
```

(Figure 3.1 using print() with and without terminator)

with the line ending set to an empty String "" the two print commands combine on one line
when we print the lines. This will be helpful later when we want successive loops of one kind
or another to combine data on one line.

Do not forget the : after terminator!

This print-function(something to print, terminator: "") is a vestige of Object-C.

18

Finally:

in the example playgrounds or projects I may have a line such as

let diamonds = 5

//diamonds = 7 //uncomment to see error

This means remove the first two // on the line

diamonds = 7 // uncomment to see error

I have always used what is called camelCaseLettering that is I write constants and variables with the first word in lowercase connected to all the rest of the words with an upper case first letter. I occasionally vary this but for the most part you can assume my variables and constants will be so named.

var howManyBananas = 3

four

Operators

Understanding Swift

In Swift operators are for the most part pretty much like the ones in C and C++. We will be using them shortly so lets look at them first.

MATH OPERATORS

= Sets one thing equal to another

+ Adds one thing to another

- Subtracts one thing to another

* Multiplies one thing by another. IT HOWEVER DOES NOT INDICATE A POINTER. No pointers in Swift.

/ Divides one thing by another

var **addition** = xInt + yInt

var **multiplication** = addition * addition

var **subtraction** = multiplication - yInt

var **division** = (subtraction * multiplication)/addition

% Modulus Operator gives the remainder when one thing is divided by another. HOWEVER in Swift you can \get the reminder of a Double divided by a Double as a Double. Whereas in C and C++ remainders were always ints. This means you need to be careful, if say you are using a Modulus Operator to determine if a result is even or odd.

```
var aDouble = 4.333                           4.333

var aDoubleToo = 5.999                         5.999

var modOfTwoDouble = aDoubleToo % aDouble      1.665999999999999
```

(Figure 4.1 using modulus on a double.)

+= Adds left item to right.

-= Subtracts left item from right.

++ at the end of a variable increase it by one. It is the equivalent of

var negtiveItem += positiveItem   (Ints only. Try it with a Double.)

— At the end of a variable decreases it by one. It is the equivalent of

      var negtiveItem -=negtiveItem   (Ints only. Try it with a Double.)

var xInt = 1

var yInt = 1

print(--xInt) //subtracts one before printing

print(yInt--) //subtracts after before print

print(yInt) //shows the subtracted one

Prints

0

1

0

Check for yourself that if we add after the above

print(++xInt)

print(yInt++)

print(yInt)

Prints

1

0

1

CONTINGENCY OPERATORS applying to Boolean Answers

|| OR operator one or the other must be as expected

&& AND operator both must be as expected

COMPARISON OPERATORS returning Boolean Values

== One thing is equal to another

>= Left side object is less than or Equal To right side.

<= Left side object is greater than or Equal To right side.

!= Things are not equal to each other

New Operators (Very specifically located. Discussed later)

? Indicates an item has no set value yet. This is called an optional value.

! A conditional somewhat similar to the ? but this says the optional value will never be nil after being given a value.

?? For a check on conditional items/

Swift also has range operators. They only work with Ints. We will see these when we get to loops. THREE is the number you should keep in mind. There are either three dots ... or two dots and one < ..<

In either case there are three characters to indicate the range choices.

"..." is called a closed range operator that includes the value on the right side of it. 1...4

"..<" is called a half-open range operator and does not include the value to the right of the <

1 ..< 4

five

Constants and Variables

Understanding Swift

In C or C++ you label the kinds of data you will work with by their kind. And end a declaration of a word or character having some value with a semicolon.

int x = 5;   const int constX = 5;

float y = 5.00; double doubleX = 5.00000000;

In Swift one of two words introduce the data factors: let and var.

Note that unlike C and C++ you do not need to add a semicolon. The end of the declaration is assumed by the return at the end of the line. You can put in semicolons if you wish.

And unlike C/C++ where you have explicitly declare what type of object you are creating, Swift can infer it by what you enter implicitly. (Yes we can cast explicitly but first:)

let creates a constant, a value that CANNOT have a different value.

For example

let myConstX = 5
is somewhat similar to
const int ConstX = 5;

var creates a variable whose value can change.
 Var x = 5
Is much like
 int x = 5;

And in both case x cannot represent something other than an int-like data object. But they are not the same. Lets look at some variables and constants in Swift.

Type the code below into your playground below

Understanding Swift

import Cocoa

var str = "Hello, playground"

Enter:

var x = 5
let myConstX = 5
var z = 5.00
var y = 5.01
var myDoubleX = 5.00000001
var mySmallDouble = .69

If you typed in the above the first thing you will have to do is fix the error. Click on the red exclamation on the left to make the error explanation appear. This explanation, however, is a little confusing. What it really means is:

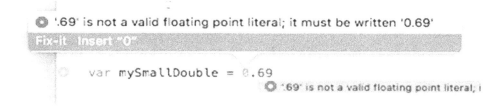

(Figure 5.1 A Double less than 1.00 one needs a 0 before the decimal.)

You need a 0 before a decimal declaration of a Double.

Try var mySmallDouble = 0.69

Understanding Swift

NOTE: I recommend you follow the example above and use camelCase capitalization for variables. That is after the first word you capitalize each additional word. For example var gMyValue = 3. This really becomes helpful as a habit when writing lots of code and trying to remember what you named something. I always use a small g in globals in C, C++ and Object C to remember they are in fact globals. Using a small g to begin the name of a global is a habit we won't really need in Swift.

Once that error has been fixed for the rest of the samples you should see something like this:

```
//: Playground - noun: a place where people can play

import Cocoa

var str = "Hello, playground"                    "Hello, playgrounc

var x = 5                                          5
let myConstX = 5                                   5
var z = 5.00                                       5
var  y = 5.01                                      5.01
var myDoubleX = 5.00000001                         5.00000001
var mySmallDouble = 0.69                           0.6899999999999
```

(Figure 5.2 the entries in our playground. Bye the way you could delete the str "Hello, playground" if you want but you need import Cocoa.)

Swift recognizes x and myConstX as Int. (Capitol I instead of small I as in the C or C++ int. Int is not quite the same as int as you will see.)

By the way if you enter the same variable name twice you will get an error. Swift like C and C++ allows only one instance of a variable. (Scope exceptions excluded.)

We will talk about switch statements later in this book. There are differences in how they work such as no need for a break; For now, I just want to show the scope differences that allow us to declare a new var x. (Not really recommended.) Using x and y from above enter this into your playground.

switch(y){

```
case 0:

    var x = 3 //this x is in a different scope than the x above


case 1:

    print(x)

default:

    print(y)
    print(x)

}
```

```
    switch(y){

    case 5.01:

        var x = 3 //this x is in a different scope than the x above      3
        print(x)                                                         "3\r

    default:

        print(y)
        print(x)

    }
```

```
3
```

(Figure 5.3 An example of a scope exception for having a variable named twice. Try changing the value y in the switch statement to something else and see what happens.)

If this seems just like C and C++ it IS NOT. An Int is not an int. A Double is not a double. Int and Double are in fact classes. They each have multiple properties. (Swift here, by the way, has designated both x and y, by the way as Doubles, not Floats. Since it cannot tell what you intended it errs on the path of caution and sets x and y each as a Double. MORE on Doubles and Floats to come.)

Bool(s) are pretty much what you'd expect. (Not quite a bool as it is also a class.) And we will be using those later on.

```
let  j:Bool = true
var  B = false
```

But there ain't no such thing as a Char or char. There is, however, a Character. Character is as close to a C/C++ "char" as you are going to come. We will get back to Character and String, as finding a Character in a String is not easy as it was in C/C+. In fact I will get back to it after, we've covered quite a few other things such as for loops, while loops, if statement and arrays. For now lets just play with numbers.

Lets try some math. Arithmetic operators + and - are pretty much the same.

```
var zPlusY = z + y
```
Gives us 10.1 in the gutter

```
var xTimesMyConstX = x*myConstX
```
You should see 25 in the gutter.

But if you try to write (i.e. change the value of myConsX)

```
myConstX = 7
```

You will get an error (Only if it is the first error. Sometimes only the first error shows. Figure 5.4). With errors the gutter is empty.

(Figure 5.4 ERROR. You cannot change a value created with let.)

Clicking on the red dot with the exclamation point will bring up the message.(Figure 5.5)

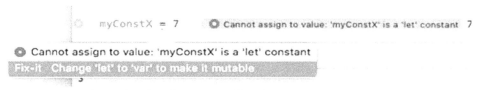

(Figure 5.5 Trying to change the value of a constant will result in an error.)

Comment the error out using two slashes //

You can also use /* */ just like in C/C++

Now try multiplying these

var yTimesZ = z*y

var MyConstXTimesZ = myConstX*z

The former works. A Double multiplied by a Double gives us a Double. But the latter (Figure 5.6) fails as a Int cannot be directly multiplied by a Double.

```
var xTimesMyConstX = x*        25
    myConstX

//myConstX = 7  //
    uncomment to see error

var yTimesZ = z*y              25.05
```

```
var MyConstXTimesZ =
    myConstX*z
    ❶ Binary operator '*' cannot be appli...
```

```
Playground execution failed: /var/folders/2j/pk_382yd4td69_gb3sk65wdr0000gn/T/.
playground2049.swift:41:30: error: binary operator '*' cannot be applied to ope
'Double'
var MyConstXTimesZ = myConstX*z
                     ---------^-
/var/folders/2j/pk_382yd4td69_gb3sk65wdr0000gn/T/./lldb/1358/playground2049.swi
overloads for '*' exist with these partially matching parameter lists: (Int, In
var MyConstXTimesZ = myConstX*z
```

(Figure 5.6 An Int multiplied by a Double fails in Swift but two Doubles can be multiplied.)

Comment out the error. Not doing so will stall the playground.

//var MyConstXTimesZ = myConstX*z

Can you somehow cast the Int to a Double and then multiply? Yes you can. Try:

//let myConstX = 5

//var z = 5.00

var myConstXTimesZInt = myConstX* Int(z)

25 should appear in the gutter. Whereas with

var zTimesMyConstXDouble = Double(myConstX)* z

I confess that when I first looked at Swift I thought they simply reversed the C/C++ casting format of (int)someFloat or (float)someInt. But no! Double() or Int() are actually functions not just simple casts. You don't need to know how they work right now. Much like you never really needed to know how strlen(word) worked in C/C++. (let o = strlen("Me") in Swift. AND BEWARE CURLEY QUOTES.)

25.05 will appear. Add the following and we'll look at the results (Figure 5.7)

var myConstXTimesYInt = myConstX * Int(y)

var yTimesMyConstXDouble = Double(myConstX)*y

var zTimesMyConstXDouble = Double(myConstX) * z

var zTimesMyConstXDouble2 = Double(myConstX) * y

var zTimesMyConstXDouble3 = Double(myConstX) * myDoubleX

```
var myConstXTimesYInt = myConstX * Int(y)

var yTimesMyConstXDouble = Double(myConstX)*y

var zTimesMyConstXDouble = Double(myConstX) * z

var zTimesMyConstXDouble2 = Double(myConstX) * y

var zTimesMyConstXDouble3 = Double(myConstX) * myDoubleX
```

Figure 5.7 in myConstXTimesZInt the result is cast to Int. But in all the rest the values are Doubles. Even for var zTimesMyConstXDouble = Double(myConstX) * z. The answer reads 25 without a period or zeros. But that 25 is a double. There are simply no significant decimals so none are shown.

Explicit vs. Implicit casting.

You can explicitly cast a variable or constant. Just introduce your variable or constant, follow it by a colon and then the type you want it to be. Try

let f:Float = 9.99

let d:Double = 9.99

let e = 9.99

var fl = f*1.0002
var dl = d*1.0002
var el = e*1.0002

The results are in (Figure 5.8) Note the difference in precision. dl has far more decimal places in the gutter. And el has the same result showing that Swift did interpret e as a Double.

```
let f:Float = 9.99              9.99

let d:Double = 9.99             9.99

let e = 9.99                    9.99

var fl = f*1.0002               9.991998
var dl = d*1.0002               9.991998000000001
var el = e*1.0002               9.991998000000001
```

(Figure 5.8 The precision of the Doubles is why Swift casts as a Double unless told otherwise.)

Did you notice as you began to type Float or Double Xcode offered a number of items that you can fill in. Let Xcode fill in Float64 for you:

let g:Float64 = 9.99

var gl = g*1.0002

Float64 is the same as a double!

Try

let a = Int.max
let b = Int64.max

Note here that Int64 or a 64 bit Int is the same as Int. There are other Int(s) Try

let a = Int.max
let aMin = Int.min

let b = Int64.max

let c = Int32.max

let q = Int32.min

let r = UInt32.max

let s = UInt.max

UInt being more or less the equivalent of an unsigned int in C/C++.

You can play with the min and max values of anything you want from UInt8.max to whatever but in the end you have to admit that the good old Int that Swift chooses allows the most bits for the buck and the largest possible numbers.

I had a old program that was written mostly in C++ that I hooked up to Object-C and made into an App. When putting it together the program started acting irregularly. What happened was that long ago I decided to use short instead of int to save space. It was that long ago that it made a difference. There was a conflict when I tried to use a short in a function that called for an int. Needless to say I changed all the shorts to ints (I could have used #define short int, but whatever) Unless you have a reason for using something like Int32 (matching a value in another program) just use Int.

Use your playground to answer these questions. It is intended for you to try this. I've hidden some things here that will expand your knowledge of Swift.

Questions

1) What is wrong with

let X = 5

let z = 5.0001

let zX = z*X

A. The X is big and z is small

B. One is a Float and the other an Int

C. One is an Int and the other a Double

D. It should be Z and x.

2) Which is a bigger number: Int.max or Int32.max or UInt16.max or UInt64.max?

A. Int.max

B. Int32.max

C. UInt16.max

D. UInt64.max

3) Which is bigger

A. UInt.max

B. UInt64.max

C. UInt8.max

D. Both A and B are the same.

4) var a = 5.0001

var b = 2

What is the correct way to multiply these two so the answer is a Double?

A. let myDouble = a*b

B. var myDouble = Int(a) * b

C. let myDouble = Double(b) * a

D. var myDouble = Int(a) * Double(b)

5) Will this work?

let germs = 0.09876

let cats = 2.00

var germyCats = germs*cats

A. Yes

B. fleas should be Fleas

C. The Double 0.09876 needs to be written as .09876

D. My cats do not have fleas.

6) How would you assign myDoubleNeg a value of -.69

a. let myDoubleNeg = -.69

b. var myDoubleNeg = .69*-1.00

c. let myDoubleNeg = -0.69

d. let myDoubleNeg = 0.69*-1

7) Which of these is the correct way to explicitly cast the variable "pounds" as a double.
Choose all that apply.

let food = 2

a. var pounds = 2.0

b. var pounds:double_t = 2

c. var pounds:Double = 2

d. var pounds = Double(food)

8) If in figure 5.3 y's value is changed to say 1.0 before it is used in the switch so that the
default prints. What value will print(x) print.

a. 5.0

b. 3

c. 3.0

d. 5.01

six

Bool Play

In your playground type:

let blue:Bool = true

let red: Int = Int(blue)

print(blue)

print(red)

```
let blue:Bool = true              true              ●
        true

let red: Int = Int(blue)          1                 ●
        1

println(blue)                     "true"            ●
        true

println(red)                      "1"              ⊕ ●
        1
```

(Figure 6.1 Not that if you push the button on the far right of the screen the values will also appear below the assignments. Also note that when print() is used for a constant or variable it is printed in quotes.) AGAIN the command "println" has been changed to "print."

Now in the above we converted a Bool blue to an Int. And found the value of it to be 1. Let's try it the other way.

let one = 1

let boolOne = Bool(one)

in the above boolOne equals true. But what about

let boolSeven = Bool(7)

this also equals true.

var boolSeven = true

let notBoolSeven = !boolSeven

here notBoolSeven will be false.

Holding your Apple key down click on the word Bool in the above. The instances and methods of the Bool class appear. We called a function Bool(7) to return the value "true" of boolSeven. You can examine Int, Float, Double etc. the same way.

try typing in:

var petite = Bool(-1)

var zero = Bool(0)

(We will be using the above in Questions below.)

What does it take to get a value of false for our Bool variables and constants? Are negative values inserted into Bool() true or false?

Bools are very handy for comparisons. Just as they are in C and C++.

```
var big = 100

var bigCopy = big

var little = 4


var resultOfComparison = big > little   //true
resultOfComparison = big == little            //false
resultOfComparison = little <= big       //true
resultOfComparison = big <= bigCopy         //true
resultOfComparison = big >= bigCopy  //true
resultOfComparison = big <= little             //false
```

Questions

1) What result will we get if we type into our playground:

 zero.description

A. an Error
B. "false"
C. same as petite.description
D. 0

2) What will be the result for var turtles here:

var turtles = Bool(-1)

A. We have no turtles.

B. false

C. true

D. We have less than one turtle

3) var liar = false

 Which of the following is equivalent.

A. var liar = Bool(28)

B. var liar = Book(-21)

C. var liar = Bool(2.444)

D. var liar = Bool(0)

4) var truly = true; var falsely = false

 var whichIsIt = truly && falsely

A. whichIsIt is true

B. whichIsIt is false

5. var truly = true; var falsely = false

 var whichIsIt = truly || falsely

A. whichIsIt is true

B. whichIsIt is false

seven

Arrays

Understanding Swift

Because of my C and C++ background when I think of an array I first think of first a string.

In Swift create a new playground but this time choose IOS instead of OS X.

The only real difference at this time will be that you will see import UIKIT instead of import Cocoa

import UIKit

var str = "Hello, playground"

char dave = "Dave"; with dave[4] being '\0'

Try typing   var dave = '\0'
Into your playground.

Sorry no '\0' in Swift. NOTE: I did not forget the first ' in '\0' above. Swift has an arrow to its location and his suggesting a change there.

There is a String "\0" and that if converted to a number they will equal nil. And there is a Character "\0" which would have to be converted to a String before it could be converted to a number, nil. But they are not quite the same as '\0' in C and C++.

You cannot create a Sting in Swift the way you do in C and C++.

var dave = "Dave"

Implicitly creates a String called dave.

But you CAN NOT access the characters in the way you would in C or C++

var firstLetter = dave[0] //gives an error message

var dave = ['D','a','v','e'] //gives the error below

(Figure 7.2 Single quotes just don't work in Swift.)

The ' is not missing. xCode removes it when it points to the space it occupies suggesting it be replaced by a ''. NO SINGLE QUOTES AND NO CURLEY QUOTES ALLOWED!

All the ' would have to be replaced by '' to get a valid Array declaration.

var dave = ["D","a","v","e"]

and dave would not be a String. In would be an array of one character Strings. This will be made clearer when we get to Strings. For now we will only discuss arrays which unlike C and C++ cannot be strings.

If we create an array of ints in C or C++ we can declare it.
int anArrayOfInts[10];

I would have ten slots to put ints in. And it would not matter when or where I did this. I could set

anArrayOfInts[2] = 7;

and get no complaint. But it would matter if I tried to put an extra int into

anArrayOfInts[11] = 2;

Because there is no anArrayOfInts[11] and that could crash my program.

IN SWIFT ARRAYS DO NOT QUITE WORK THAT WAY! AND WE ARE BETTER OFF STARTING FROM SCRATCH IN OUR THINKING. Think of Arrays (note the capitol A) in Swift like train cars that can be filled with anything you want. And Strings, well they need to be thought of so quite differently than Arrays, that we will cover Strings later on.

First Only one type of element is allowed in an Array.

var biElementArray = ["Mom", 7]

THIS IS AN ERROR! BUT IT WOULD NOT BE RECOGNIZED AS AN ERROR. This would actually appear to be okay in your playground, however, Swift does not consider this an array. If we declare biElementArray as an Array of Strings. In either of two ways.

var biElementArray = Array<String>() //an Array of type Sting
//or
var biElementArray = [String]() //String in [] signifies an Array.

You should see the empty array symbol [] in the gutter. If you put both of these into a playground at the same time one will fail with an error as you cannot identify a variable with the same name twice.

And then write:

biElementArray = ["Mom", 7]

We will get an Error. As we would if comment out the above and we enter:

var biElementArray:[Int] = ["Mom", 7] //Error
Whereas the declaration below will work.

var aRealArray:[Int] = [5, 7]

The reason for this is type safety. Swift prevents you from using the wrong type of data. Thus:

Arrays only have one kind of element.

Let's imagine we want an array of ten ints and only ten ints and the items in the array will be constant and not ever change. Here is how we'd do this in Swift implicitly.

let anArrayOfInts = [0,1,2,3,4,5,6,7,8,9]

Arrays as in C and C++ always start their position numbering with 0.
So if we want to change a value we'd do it like this.

AnArrayOfInts[0] = 10

Try typing them in and you'll get a error. Of course we'd first have to change let above to var first if we want a mutable array.

```
var str = "Hello, playground"              "Hello, playground

var anArrayOfInts = [0,1,2,3,4,5,6,       [0, 1, 2, 3, 4, 5, 6, 7
    7,8,9]

anArrayOfInts[0]      Cannot assign throu...  10
    = 10
```

Cannot assign through subscript: 'anArrayOfInts' is a 'let' constant

Fix-it Change 'let' to 'var' to make it mutable

(Figure 7.3 We introduced this array with let. These values are constants.)

Isn't it nice that Xcode tells us what we did wrong and how to correct it.

var anArrayOfInts = [0,1,2,3,4,5,6,7,8,9]
AnArrayOfInts[0] = 10

And to print out our changed array we'll add

Print(AnArrayOfInts)

Understanding Swift

To see the results of your print click on the right top of the page in the little rectangle with the line on the bottom.

Now try typing in :

anArrayOfInts[0] = 0

anArrayOfInts[11] = 10

```
anArrayOfInts[0] = 0                    0
anArrayOfInts[11] = 10  //             10
    uncomment to see the error
    in the output area below.
    This goes beyond the range
    of the array.

anArrayOfInts

print( anArrayOfInts)
```

```
[10, 1, 2, 3, 4, 5, 6, 7, 8, 9]
fatal error: Array index out of range
Playground execution failed: Execution was interrupted, reason: EXC
(code=EXC_I386_INVOP, subcode=0x0).
* thread #1: tid = 0x8bc68, 0x000000010ef4c258 libswiftCore.dylib`f
```

(Figure 7.5 OOPS we get a fatal Error

Swift knows that we set up our mutable array for ten items. So how do we add items?)

Lets try two ways.

anArrayOfInts.append(11) //works

anArrayOfInts += [12]

anArrayOfInts += 12 crashes and gives an error

Keep in mind this rule.

anArrayOfInts[11] = 5   //works

anArrayofInts += [13] // works and adds a 13th item

aStringArray = ["ma","my","mo"] //Beware of smart quotes!

If there are brackets the left side of the = sign there are none on the right and vice versa.

Lets switch to an Array of Strings.

aStringArray += ["mum"] //works

aStringArray[0] = "me" //works

If we introduce an Array but do not immediately give it values: var aNewIntArray = [Int]()

   var anotherNewIntArray = Array<Int>()

   var aNewStringArray = Array<String>()

   var anotherNewStringArray = [Array]()

```
var  aNewIntArray  = [Int]()                            []
var  anotherNewIntArray  = Array<Int>()                 []
var aNewStringArray = Array<String>()                   []
var anotherNewStringArray = [String]()                  []

aNewIntArray = [0,1,2,3,4,5,6,7,8,9]                    [0, 1, 2, 3, 4, 5, 6, 7, 8, 9]

aNewIntArray += [10]                                   [0, 1, 2, 3, 4, 5, 6, 7, 8, 9, 10]

aNewStringArray = ["ma","my","mo"]                     ["ma", "my", "mo"]

aNewStringArray += ["mum"]                             ["ma", "my", "mo", "mum"]
aNewStringArray[0] = "me" //note the quotes            "me"
print(aNewIntArray)                                    "[0, 1, 2, 3, 4, 5, 6, 7, 8, 9, 10]\n"
```

▶

[0, 1, 2, 3, 4, 5, 6, 7, 8, 9, 10]

(Figure 7.6 What does aNewStringArray look like after add aNewStringArray[0] = "me" ?)

In your playground try this. Click on the word Array as in Array<Int>() and look at the possible ways to use your new array. Here are some below.

var **kot** = Array<String>()

`kot = ["What","is"]

//By holding the apple command down with your cursor Array you will see extensions
available

```
//By holding the apple command down with your cursor Array you will see
    extensions available
kot.append("name")                                    ["What","is","name"]
kot += ["please"]                                      ["What","is","name","please"]
kot.count                                              4
kot.capacity                                           4
kot.insert("your", atIndex: 2) //indexes always start with zero    ["What","is","your","name","please"]
kot += ["stupid!"]                                     ["What","is","your","name","please","stupid!"]
kot.removeLast()                                       "stupid!"
kot                                                    ["What","is","your","name","please"]
kot.removeAtIndex(4)                                   "please"
```

(Figure 7.7 Ways to add and subtract items from an array.)

kot.count gives us how many items are in our array. We will be using this in our loops
section.

When we talk about loops we'll discuss moving through, and printing out our arrays.

Questions: Hold down the command key while holding the cursor on Array and find the
answers to these questions in the extensions.

1. What is result here?

var result = kot + aStringArray

a. "Fee Fi Fo Fum"

b. ["ma","my","mo","What", "is", "your", "name"]

c. ERROR

d. ["What", "is", "your", "name", "me", "my", "mo","mum"]

2 For aNewIntArray above what would

aNewIntArray.isEmpty

return.

a. true

b. false

c. nil

3 For aNewIntArray type in

aNewIntArray.insert(-1, atIndex: 0)

now if you try

aNewIntArray.popLast()

what will be returned

a. -1

b. 4

c. 10

d. 1

4. How would you use this Array extension in your playground

public init(count: Int, repeatedValue: Element)

5. What is an easy way to remove everything from your kot array?

a. kot.removeAll()

b. kot.capacity = 0

C. kot = nil

6. Can Arrays contain different types of elements.

a. Yes

b. No

c. Depends

7) var someElementTypeArray:[What goes here to make this a valid Array] = ["My", "Mom"]

Answers:

1. d

2. b. false

3. c. 10

4.   var list = Array<Int>(count: 4, repeatedValue: 6)

          var list2 = [Int](count: 5, repeatedValue: 7)

5. a. kot.removeAll()

6. b. Arrays elements must all be the same.

eight

If else

Understanding Swift

There really isn't any need in an if statement to mention then. So Swift doesn't have a then or even need (). And since the if statements work much like they do in C and C++ with only minor differences we'll go through those differences quickly.

An if statement has a conditional statement and if that statement resolves* as true it executes the instructions for a "true" return.
(* note I didn't say "is" true as that implies your data, etc, is correct.)

An if statement in Swift is ALWAYS followed by brackets
```
if (true)
{
          //the magic happens
}
```

Below we may buy candy.   If there are other possibilities we may add an else statement.
UNLIKE C and C++ you must have brackets.

```
var pennies = 5
let enoughToBuyCandy = 5
if pennies >= enoughToBuyCandy{

   print("We may buy candy!")
}


var numberOfPenniesString = "pennies"

pennies = 4

if enoughToBuyCandy - pennies == 1{

   numberOfPenniesString = "penny"
```

```
}

if pennies >= enoughToBuyCandy{

    print("We can may candy!")

} else {

    print("We go home candy less \(enoughToBuyCandy - pennies) \(numberOfPenniesString)
short.")

}
```

AND WE GET: We go home candy less 1 penny short

And as in C and C++ we can have an else if.

```
 pennies = 7

if enoughToBuyCandy - pennies == 1{

    numberOfPenniesString = "penny"
}

if pennies == enoughToBuyCandy{

    print("We may buy candy!")

} else if pennies > enoughToBuyCandy {

    print("We may get \( pennies - enoughToBuyCandy) pennies worth more of candy.")
```

```
}else{

    print("We go home candy less \(enoughToBuyCandy - pennies) \(numberOfPenniesString)
short.")
}
```

AND WE GET: We may get 2 pennies worth more of candy.

Understanding Swift

```
var pennies = 5                                    5
let enoughToBuyCandy = 5                            5
if pennies >= enoughToBuyCandy{

    print("We may buy candy!")                     "We may buy candy!\n"
}


var numberOfPenniesString = "pennies"              "pennies"

pennies = 4                                        4

if enoughToBuyCandy - pennies == 1{

    numberOfPenniesString = "penny"                "penny"
}

if pennies >= enoughToBuyCandy{

    print("We can may candy!")

} else {

    print("We go home candy less \                 "We go home candy less 1
        (enoughToBuyCandy - pennies) \
        (numberOfPenniesString) short.")

}

pennies = 7                                        7

if enoughToBuyCandy - pennies == 1{

    numberOfPenniesString = "penny"
}

if pennies == enoughToBuyCandy{

    print("We may buy candy!")

} else if pennies > enoughToBuyCandy {

    print("We may get \( pennies -                 "We may get 2 pennies wc
        enoughToBuyCandy) pennies worth
        more of candy.")

}else{

    print("We go home candy less \
        (enoughToBuyCandy - pennies) \
        (numberOfPenniesString) short.")
```

(Figure 8.1 Pennies manipulated with if else.)

nine

Optionals

Optionals

What are optionals? In your playground type in:

var **lemons** = Int?()

var **limes** = Int!()

var **peaches** = 5

lemons = 5

limes = 5

lemons = nil

limes = nil

peaches = nil

The last item peaches = nil will generate an ERROR. Only conditionals can have a nil value. That is *nil* is no value at all.

Unlike other languages in Swift a nil is not a pointer to a nonexistent object. That is we can think of pointers in C and C++ as being like a library reference card. Imagine a library where you have a card file—like the old days where paper cards in an alphabetically organized drawer listed the book's location. And the book was on a shelf organized by the Dewey Decimal System. A pointer is like the library reference card and it points to the books location. The book is like a value at that location.

In a real library the book can be gone with the card in the file. In C and C++ a filled out card **MUST** always point to a spot on the shelf and the book must be there or we invite disaster. For programming example in C++ that may refresh this in your mind check out the next section. If you don't feel you need a refresher skip to the following section.

```
    var peaches = 5
❶   peaches = nil
```

```
    ▶
```

```
Playground execution failed: /var/folders/2j/pk_382yd4td69_gb3sk65wdr0
/lldb/1282/playground1780.swift:22:11: error: nil cannot be
assigned to type 'Int'
peaches = nil
```

(Figure 9.1 Once set with a value peaches can't be nil)

Understanding Swift

If you are up on your C or C++ and are clear on how a pointer can cause a crash you can skip ahead to the next chapter. Otherwise enjoy this refresher.

Create a new console project.

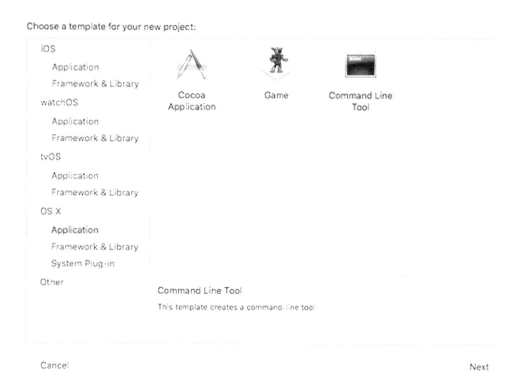

(Figure 9.2 Set up a Command Line tool Project.)

I've named mine libraryCardAndFileTest. You can name yours whatever you wish.

Choose options for your new project:

Product Name: libraryCardAndFileTest

Organization Name: David Francis Curran

Organization Identifier: DFCurranproductions

Bundle Identifier: DFCurranproductions.libraryCardAndFileTest

Language: C++

Cancel   Previous   Next

(Figure 9.3 Name Your Project.)

Click Next, confirm the location and you should see this:

```
//
//   main.cpp
//   libraryCardAndFileTest
//
//   Created by David Curran on 12/6/15.
//   Copyright © 2015 David Francis Curran. All rights reserved.
//

#include <iostream>

int main(int argc, const char * argv[]) {
    // insert code here...
    std::cout << "Hello, World!\n";
    return 0;
}
```

after

#include <iostream>

add

using namespace std;

Then delete the highlighted section and replace with the code below within the /////... breaks below.

(be sure, after pasting to delete the credits at the bottom.)

///

int **book** = 1999334; //we have put a book # 1999334 on the shelf.

int *libraryCardPtr = &book; //This is our library reference card pointing to our book. &book is the shelf location of book

```
cout << "*libraryCardPtr is: " << *libraryCardPtr << " the book itself.\nlibraryCardPtr == "
<< libraryCardPtr << " is the books location in memory. \nand book == " << book << " the
book itself same as *libraryCardPtr\n\n"; // value pointed to by pointer


    libraryCardPtr = 0; //we set the library card to blank
    cout << "Now we will set libraryCardPtr to zero.  libraryCardPtr = " << libraryCardPtr <<
"\n\n";


    cout << "Because libraryCardPtr is Null referencing *libraryCardPtr would cause a crash
and so cannot be referenced. \n libraryCardPtr == " << libraryCardPtr << "\nand book == "
<< book << " it is still on the shelf but is no longer pointed to by the card. The card is blank.
\n\n"; // value pointed to by pointer

    cout << "We would get an ERROR if we try to locate the book via the card as the card
libraryCardPtr = " <<libraryCardPtr <<  " \n\n";


        return 0;


//////////////////////////////////////////////////////////////////////



Putting a blank card in the file (yet to be filed out) is like a null pointer.
If there is no book, the card is blank, the pointer points to a location where nothing is there.
And in C and C++ referencing a null pointer can crash a program.

    int *cardForBookYetToBeEntered = 0;


    cout << "cardForBookYetToBeEntered = " << cardForBookYetToBeEntered << " a blank
card. \n\n";
```

Trying to do the line below:

cout << *cardForBookYetToBeEntered; //will cause an error

The above example is similar to a library where the book has not been removed but the library reference card no long points to it. Try adding the code below to your libraryCardAndFileTest C++ project

before the:

return 0.

```
/////////////////////////////////////////
int size = 1;

int *intBlockPtr = (int*)malloc(size*sizeof( int ));


cout << *intBlockPtr << " = intBlockPtr\n\n";

*intBlockPtr += 10000789;  //we have created shelf space and added book 10000789

cout << "*intBlockPtr == " << *intBlockPtr << "\n\n";

cout << "intBlockPtr == " << intBlockPtr << "\n\n";


cout << "Now we free( intBlockPt\n\n"; //we have deleted the shelves and floor

free(intBlockPtr);
```

cout << " intBlockPtr = "<< **intBlockPtr** << "\n\n"; // the pointer still points at the location

//but the complier thinks the block is free. Here is this small program the line below might still work. However. the complier could write something else there with disastrous results.

cout << " *intBlockPtr = "<< ***intBlockPtr** << "\n\n";

///

    return 0;

///

Understanding Swift

Asking for the book at a location that has been erased can cause an error.

Pointing to a spot that has been deallocated in memory is like sending someone to a library reference card location where the shelf is gone and where they will fall through the floor.

In C and C++ each book requires a reference card and a shelf space. In our analogy both take up memory.

In Swift, however, a **var**(iable) set to nil means it has NO VALUE of any kind yet. Swift does not have pointers. It is like not having library reference cards at all. Nil tells you that the book does not exist, period.

What about constant values? Try setting **let** dogs = Int!() and see what happens. One of those little red error circles with a solution will come up when you try to set dogs to some real value and let will be changed for you to **var**. Constants cannot be optionals.

Lets play a bit with optionals. Referencing a nil value will cause problems. How can we use optionals to prevent that? There is a lot to understand here, so bear with me if you have questions until the end.

Lets imagine you don't know what a value is when you start out. You have 1 dollar but don't know how many apples you can buy for that $1.

var apples = Int?() //note this used to not have the () at the end but that has been changed.

if apples >= 1{

    print("We have \(apples)")

} else {

    print("We ain't got no apples today!")

71

```
var apples = Int?()   //note this used to      nil
    not have the () at the end but that has
    been changed.

if apples >= 1{

    print("We have \(apples)")

} else {   //this covers all else including
       nil

    print("We ain't got no apples today!")      "We ain't got n
```

}

(Figure 9.4 Avoiding a value equal to nil.)

Note that the in the gutter var apples is given a value of nil. And that the if else knows that nil is not greater than or equal to 1.

But what if continuing from that you add.

let applesPerCrate = 20

var appleCratesNeeded = apples/applesPerCrate

```
let applesPerCrate = 20          20

var appleCratesNeeded =
    apples/applesPerCrate //
    uncomment to see error
    and suggested
    correction.
```

```
Playground execution failed: /var/folders/2j/pk_382yd4td69_gb3sk65wdr0000
playground2011.swift:15:25: error: value of optional type 'Int?' not unwr
to use '!' or '?'?
var appleCratesNeeded - apples/applesPerCrate //uncomment to see error an
correction.
```

(Figure 9.5 Swift complains bout an unwrapped value.)

We get an error. The circle with the dot in the center error indicates that if we click on it, it will show us possible fixes for the error. This is as opposed to the exclamation point in a circle which does not offer possible changes.

(Figure 9.6 Clicking on the red circle for further info.)

Above a solution is presented if we click on the lower circle with a white dot.

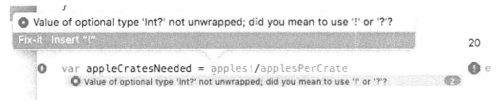

(Figure 9.7 Exploring the error even further.)

Clicking on the blue Fix-it Solution will result in the line changing to:

var appleCratesNeeded = apples!/applesPerCrate

Note the insertion of a ! after apples and before the division slash /. This is called a forced unwrapping. However this, as written (because apples are nil) also fatally crashes.

What does it mean when the program says that "Value of optional type 'Int?' is not unwrapped? Well very simply:

var potatoes = 1

Implicitly casts potatoes as an Int. That is the program assumes potatoes is an Int.

var motatoes = Double(1)

Explicitly casts potatoes as an Double.

var apples = Int?() Explicitly casts apples as an Int but the value of apples has not been unwrapped.

var appleCratesNeeded = apples/applesPerCrate

In the above apples has not been unwrapped. But it needs to be so Swift asks above do you want to unwrap apples.

```
var appleCratesNeeded = apples/applesPerCrate                          error
          Value of optional type 'Int?' not unwrapped; did you mean to use '!' or '?'?
```
(Figure 9.8 You are asked if you want to unwrap apples.)

To do so you write it this way.

var appleCratesNeeded = apples!/applesPerCrate

var pears = Int!()

Explicitly states that pears is an "unwrapped" Int. because it is explicitly unwrapped you could write:

var pearCratesNeeded = pears/applesPerCrate

without an exclamation mark needed after pears.

We'll show you how to make a forced unwrapping work soon. First I want to show what Swift will do in various circumstances.

```
let applesPerCrate = 20                                                20
var appleCratesNeeded = apples!/applesPerCrate                         error
    Execution was interrupted, reason: EXC_BAD_INSTRUCTION (code=EXC_I386_INVOP, subco...
```
(Figure 9.9 apples is unwrapped but where is its unwrapped value?)

So lets start over. Using oranges var oranges = Int!() Here we've used ! instead of ?.

This mean that oranges is declared explicitly as an Int and explicitly as an unwrapped optional. Lets say we declared pennies to be

var **pennies** = 21

```
var oranges = Int!() //note this used to not have the () at the    nil
    end but that has been changed.

let orangesPerCrate = 20                                             20

if pennies >= 100 {

    oranges = 5
}

if oranges >= 1{                                                    error
    Execution was interrupted, reason: EXC_BAD_INSTRUCTION (code=EXC_I386_INVOP,...
    print("We have \(oranges)")

} else {

    print("We ain't got no oranges today!")

}
```

(Figure 9.10 oranges only gets a value if pennies >= 100. It needs a value for all cases the program crashes.)

We see our fatal error shows before it can execute at all. Having a nil value show up where a real value is needed can cause our programs to crash.

Lets see how we can use it correctly. If we type in the below will it work?

var **today** = "Tuesday"

var **plums** = Int?()

if today == "Tuesday" {

   plums = 8

}

var **plumsPerDay** = plums * 1

No. We will get a self correcting error message:

```
    var today = "Tuesday"                                    Tuesday

    var plums = Int?()                                       nil

    if today == "Tuesday" {

        plums = 8                                            8
    }
○   var plumsPerDay = plums * 1                              8
```

(Figure 9.11 What is wrong here? plums need to be unwrapped!)

If we click on the red circle we get:

```
        if today == "Tuesday" {
  ● Value of optional type 'Int?' not unwrapped; did you mean to use '!' or '?'?
  Fix-it  Insert "!"

        var plumsPerDay = plums! * 1
                    ● Value of optional type 'Int?' not unwrapped; did you mean to use '!' or '
```

(Figure 9.12 Clicking on the red circle tells us what is needed.)

It tell us to insert a ! after plums in the last line.

```
var today = "Tuesday"                                    "Tuesday"
var plums = Int?()                                       nil
if today == "Tuesday" {
    plums = 8                                            8
}
var plumsPerDay = plums! * 1                             8
```

(Figure 9.13 We've unwrapped plums and out code works.)

Inserting a ! fixes the problem. It tell us to unwrap our inexplicit

var plums = Int?()

before using it.

One thing we can do about about optionals in our programs is prevent errors with the nil coalescing operator: ?? . The ?? choses between an object that may be nil and an alternate. Below we'll choose between oranges and 0.

var oranges = Int!() //note this used to not have the () at the end but that has been changed.

var numberOfOranges = oranges ?? 0 //Here we set numberOfOranges to oranges if oranges is not nil and 0 if oranges is equal to nil.

print(numberOfOranges)

if numberOfOranges >= 1{

   print("We have \(oranges)")

} else {

```
    print("We ain't got no oranges today!")

}
```

We can also do it this way with an if else.

```
if oranges != nil {


    print("We have \(oranges)")

} else {

    print("We ain't got no oranges today!")

}
```

A random number is just one of a multitude of items that can be used to validate our conditionals.

```
    var bananas = Int?() //Explicitly an Int but this will not force unwrapped.

    bananas = Int(arc4random_uniform(12)+ 1) //sets bananas to a random number.
between one and twelve

    /*


    arc4random_uniform(12) sets bananas to a random UInt32 value between 0 and 11.  By
adding +1 to it (inside the Int() function) we get a random number between 1 and 12.
```

bananas needs to be cast to an Int so we use the function Int() and throw our random number generator into it.

And we need to unwrap bananas with a !

*/

```
print("We have \(bananas!) bananas that is \((Double(bananas!)/12.00*100.0)) % of a dozen")
```

Questions:

1)As written the code below will result in a fatal error. What would need to be added to the first else{ } below to avoid a fatal error.

```
var numberOfBananas = Int!() //note this used to not have the () at the end but that has been changed.

var nickles = 5

if nickles == 6 {

    numberOfBananas = 3

} else{

    //add something here to keep this code from crashing
}
```

```
print(numberOfBananas)

if numberOfBananas >= 1{

    print("We have \(numberOfBananas) bananas")

} else {

    print("We ain't got no numberOfBananas today!")
}
```

Answer:

```
} else{

    numberOfBananas = nickles/2
    //or any other result that will always gives numberOfBananas  a value.
}
```

ten

For and In Loops

Understanding Swift

Begin a new playground for OS X. I called mine myLoopPlayground.

For loops are in many ways the same for Swift as they are in C and C++.

```
for( int i = 4; i < 10; i++){

    cout << i << "\n";   //This is a C++ loop
}
```

However the for loop in Swift needs only brackets. We can declare the variable inside or outside the loop.

```
for var i = 4.0; i < 7; i++ {
    print(i)
    print("i == \(i) \n")
}
```

```
for var i = 4.0; i < 7; i++ {
        print(i)
        print("i == \(i) \n")

    }
```

```
4.0
i == 4.0

5.0
i == 5.0

6.0
i == 6.0
```

(Figure 10.1 i set to a double stays a double.)

And yes we can use Doubles as our variable.

If you wish you can write the for loop the C way.

var i:double_t = 1
for(i = 0; i < 4; i++){

        //do something for each value of i

}

But you may not do this:

```
var x:double_t = 1
for( x = 0; x < 4; x++)
    print(x)  //this will generator an error indicating you need to add brackets.
```

To fix the loop add brackets

```
        var x:double_t = 0
        for( x = 0; x < 4; x++){
          print(x)
        }
```

and we get these results:

0.0

1.0

2.0

3.0

Remember the range operators mentioned in the the operators chapter? We can use them to write a simple loop. The increments here are assumed to be Ints and the increase one in each case.

```
for i in 4 ..< 7 {  //This uses the half-open range operator ..<
  for j in 7...10 {  //This uses the closed range operator …
      print("\(i) \(j)")
  }
}
```

gives us

4 7

4 8

4 9

4 10

5 7

5 8

5 9

5 10

6 7

6 8

6 9

Moving through the loop is call iteration. And you may be used to using an index, say the location of something in an Array of Strings to print out the Array.

```
var myLoopArray = ["My","very", "eager","mother","just","served","up","nine","pies"]

var y = 0  //implicitly defined as Int

for( y = 0; y < 4; y++){
   print("myLoopArray[\(y)] == \(myLoopArray[y])")
}
```

And we get:

myLoopArray[0] == My

myLoopArray[1] == very

myLoopArray[2] == eager

myLoopArray[3] == mother

But that is not our whole array. Well Swift gives us an easy way to access the entire array without having to remember how many items we have in it. Lets add a newly written loop. Remember "count"?

```
myLoopArray.count
    gives us 8

var y:Int

for( y = 0; y < myLoopArray.count; y++) {
   print("myLoopArray[\(y)] == \(myLoopArray[y])")
}
```

Gives us all the planets. (If you don't understand this reference look up the sentence formed by these words online. I programmed a few Mac Apps I had written originally in C++ or C by learning just enough Object-C to get by. When I got stuck I asked a question in a Google search. I found how to do what I needed to do every time. You might have to look more than once, and reword your question, but I was able to find an answer to every question I had.)

```
var myLoopArray = ["My","very",                              ["M
    "eager","mother","just","served","up","nine",            eage
    "pies"]                                                   just'
                                                              nine

var y = 0  //implicitly defined as Int                       0

for( y = 0; y < 4; y++){
    print("myLoopArray[\(y)] == \                            (4 ti
        (myLoopArray[y])")
}

myLoopArray.count                                            9

for( y = 0; y < myLoopArray.count; y++) {
    print("myLoopArray[\(y)] == \                            (9 ti
        (myLoopArray[y])")
}

for planet in myLoopArray.enumerate() {

    print(planet)                                            (9 ti
}

for planet in myLoopArray {

    print(planet)                                            (9 ti
}
```

▽ ▶

```
myLoopArray[0] == My        (0, "My")       My
myLoopArray[1] == very      (1, "very")     very
myLoopArray[2] == eager     (2, "eager")    eager
myLoopArray[3] == mother    (3, "mother")   mother
myLoopArray[0] == My        (4, "just")     just
myLoopArray[1] == very      (5, "served")   served
myLoopArray[2] == eager     (6, "up")       up
myLoopArray[3] == mother    (7, "nine")     nine
myLoopArray[4] == just      (8, "pies")     pies
myLoopArray[5] == served
myLoopArray[6] == up
```

(Figure 10.2 One way to print out all the array members with index showing: A tradition for loop. Note printout is edited via photoshop.)

NOTE I used var y:Int to introduce variable y. Could I have made y a conditional?

No both var y = Int?() and Int!() fail because as your Swift playground will tell you:

error: unary operator '++' cannot be applied to an operand of type '@lvalue Int!' (aka '@lvalue ImplicitlyUnwrappedOptional<Int>')

Enter into your playground:

```
for planet in myLoopArray.enumerate() {

    print(planet)
}
```

enumerate() will give the index with your array item. Note that enumerate(myLoopArray) is no longer correct.

(0, "My")

(1, "very")

(2, "eager")

(3, "mother")

(4, "just")

(5, "served")

(6, "up")

(7, "nine")

(8, "pies")

For in Loops

But the nice thing about Swift is we don't need a reference index to iterate though an Array. We can use what is called fast enumeration.

We can loop through myLoopArray in a different way by using a for-in-loop.

```
for planet in myLoopArray {

    print(planet)
}
```

I didn't have to use the name "planet". I could have used "word", or "item", or "memory-helper".

But the for-in-loop tells Swift to use whatever name I have after for as meaning an index to the elements in the Array. The word after "in" has to be the name of the Array.

```
for planet in myLoopArray {

    print(planet)
}
```

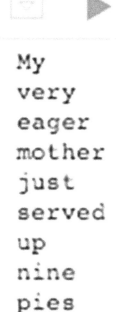

```
My
very
eager
mother
just
served
up
nine
pies
```

(Figure 10.3 using the for in loop to print our planets.)

You don't need to worry about count in this kind of loop because the for-in-loop figures that out for you. We can use fast enumeration for more than just arrays. We'll show you how when we cover those other types.

Questions:

Using myLoopArray above what will

```
for indice in 4...7 {

    print(myLoopArray[indice])
}
```

we get:

1) Nothing this fails

2)   just
      served
      up
      nine

3) 4,5,6,7

4) just
   served
   up

eleven

While Loops

Understanding Swift

Like C and C++ Swift has both while loops and ~~do while~~ repeat-while loops.

In C we might write for a while loop

```
int x = 0;
while( x < 6){  //Asserts a condition to be met

    printf("We are on the verge of breakthrough%d!\n",x); //does something we need done.
    x++;  //gives us a way to exit the loop.
}
```

//OR for a do-while loop

```
    x = 100;

do{
    printf("We are on the verge of breakthrough%d!\n",x); //does something we need done.
    x++;  //gives us a way to exit the loop.

}while( x < 6);
```

whereas in Swift it would be.

```
var x = 0
while x < 6 {

    print("We are on the verge of a breakthrough\(x)")
    x++
}
//and

x = 100
```

Understanding Swift

repeat { // repeat is now used instead of do in SWIFT

  print("We are on the verge of a breakthrough\(x)")

  x += 100

}while x < 8 //we need to make sure the while loop ends at some time.

In both cases we get something like

```
import Cocoa

var x = 0                                                    0
while x < 6 {

    print("We are on the verge of a breakthrough\(x)")    (6 times)
    x++                                                   (6 times)
}

x = 100                                                    100

repeat {

    print("We are on the verge of a breakthrough\(x)")   "We are on the verge o
    x += 100                                              200

}while x < 8
```

```
We are on the verge of a breakthrough0
We are on the verge of a breakthrough1
We are on the verge of a breakthrough2
We are on the verge of a breakthrough3
We are on the verge of a breakthrough4
We are on the verge of a breakthrough5
We are on the verge of a breakthrough100
```

(Figure 11.1 using a while loop.)

Note that the repeat{…..}while loop here ran only once. The repeat loop will always work at least once no matter what the condition(s) set. The while may not run at all depending on the conditions set.

twelve

Switches

Understanding Swift

Switch statements in C or C++ are very similar to those in Swift with some slightly different conventions.

```
int dog = 5;

switch(dog)
{
case 0:
  printf("Boxer");
  break;  //breaks are necessary after each unless you want to run them together
case 2:
  printf("Irish Setter");
  break;
case 3:
  printf("Doberman");
  break;
case 4:
  printf("Springer Spaniel");
  break;
case 5:
                    printf("Unknown "); //no break and these combine
default:
  printf("Mutt");
}
printf("\n\n");
```

will print out "Unknown Mutt".

In Swift we would have In Swift switch statements must be exhausted. You do not always need a

```
default:
```

Understanding Swift

but you do need to have an exhaustive list in you switch statement.

Consider

```
var trueOrFalse = true

switch(trueOrFalse){

case true:

    print("true")

case false:

    print("false")

}
```

This is exhaustive. True and false are the only possible Bool replies and both are covered so it does indeed work.

```
var trueOrFalse = true                                    true

switch(trueOrFalse){

case true:

    print("true")                                        "true\

case false:

    print("false")


}
```

(Figure 12.1 An exhaustive switch, No other replies are possible so this is exhaustive.)

What about the following?

```
var trueOrFalse = "blue"

switch(trueOrFalse){

case "true":

   print("true")

case "false":

   print("false")


}
```

Understanding Swift

In this example the replies are not exhaustive.

```
var trueOrFalse = "blue"

switch(trueOrFalse){

case "true":

    print("true")

case "false"

    print("false")

}          Switch must be exhaustive, consider adding a defau
```

(Figure 12.2 We don't know if blue is true or false so the search is not exhaustive.)

We actually get a warning that our switch is not exhaustive.

```
var trueOrFalse = "blue"

switch(trueOrFalse){

case "true":

  print("true")
```

```
case "false":

    print("false")

default:

    print("false")

}
```

By Adding a default we make the above exhaustive.

```
var trueOrFalse = "blue"          "b

switch(trueOrFalse){

case "true":

    print("true")

case "false":

    print("false")

default:

    print ("false")              "fa

}
```

(Figure 12.3 We have a default so the search is exhaustive.)

So with switch in Swift you do not need a default if your list of replies is otherwise exhaustive.

As in C and C++ switch statements can be easier to write and read than long if else combinations.

If your user input is a String a switch statement can make possible answers easier.

Create a new Swift console project rather than a playground

(Figure 12.4 Save a console project (Command Line Tool).)

I have saved mine as switchByEnteredString.

Choose options for your new project:

Product Name:	switchByEnteredString	
Organization Name:	David Francis Curran	
Organization Identifier:	DFCurranproductions	
Bundle Identifier:	DFCurranproductions.switchByEnteredString	
Language:	Swift	⌄

Cancel   Previous   Next

(Figure 12.5 Name your project and hit next. Then Create on the next screen.)

Click Next, make sure it is in the file you want it to be in and click create.

Then open the main.swift file

Open main.swift

(Figure 12.6 Open main.swift.)

And enter the code below. After where the name and copyright info is commented out. I have made var reply a conditional String that is forced unwrapped. Then used the coalescing operator just in case noting gets entered. We have not discussed functions yet so that part of this will be discussed later. For now just use the code here.

```
————————————————————————————————————————————

//
// main.swift
// switchByEnteredString
//
// Created by David Curran on 12/8/15.
// Copyright © 2015 David Francis Curran. All rights reserved.
//

import Foundation

func userEnteredData() -> String{

    let userTypedIn = NSFileHandle.fileHandleWithStandardInput()
```

```swift
    let myEnteredString = userTypedIn.availableData
    return NSString(data: myEnteredString, encoding:NSUTF8StringEncoding) as! String
}
print( "Please enter your gender")

var reply = String!()

reply = userEnteredData()

var replyForSwitch  = reply ?? "Error "  //nil coalescing operator to prevent an error.


switch(replyForSwitch){

case "Error":

   print("There has been a ERROR please try again!")

case "Male","M","MALE","m": //spelling counts so try for all possibilities

   print( "Thank you sir!")
default:  //if you are not male…
   print( "Thank you ma'am'!")


}
```

——

Here is the output. As you can see below I've entered male but was thanked as a ma'am. Why did this error occur?

Understanding Swift

Understanding Swift

```
import Foundation

func userEnteredData() -> String{

    let userTypedIn = NSFileHandle.fileHandleWithStandardInput()

    let myEnteredString = userTypedIn.availableData

    return NSString(data: myEnteredString, encoding:NSUTF8StringE
        String
}
print( "Please enter your gender")

var reply = String!()

reply = userEnteredData()

var replyForSwitch  = reply ?? "Error "   //nil coalescing operato
    an error.


switch(replyForSwitch){

case "Error":

    print("There has been a ERROR please try again!")


 //this is the corrected case below

case "Male","M","MALE","m","male":

    print( "Thank you sir!")
default:   //if you are not male…
    print( "Thank you ma'am'!")

}
```

```
Hello, World!
Please enter your gend
male
Thank you ma'am'!
Program ended with exi
```

(Figure 12.7 We get an error if we indicate male. Why?)

Double check yourself. Enter male in any of the ways offered and your reply will be "Thank you ma'am'!" Why?

Lets set some break points and solve again.

```
print( "Please enter your gender")

var reply = String!()

reply = userEnteredData()

var replyForSwitch  = reply ?? "Error "  //nil coalescing operator to preve

switch(replyForSwitch){

case "Error":

    print("There has been a ERROR please try again!")

case "Male","M","MALE","m": //spelling counts so try for all possibilities

    print( "Thank you sir!")
default:  //if you are not male...
    print( "Thank you ma'am'!")

}
```

switchByEnteredString   Thread 1   0 main

▶ reply = (String) "Male\n"
▶ replyForSwitch = (String) "Male\n"
▶ Exception State Registers
▶ Floating Point Registers
▶ General Purpose Registers
  $match (String)
  $match (String)
  $match (String)
  $match (String)
  $match (String)

Please enter your gender
Male
(lldb)

Here is the error there
end of our entry.

(Figure 12.8 The error is caused by a "\n" at the end of our reply.)

This reminds me of input problems when I was starting out learning C. Here Swift collected what the user entered including the \n at the end

And easy correction change

case Male","M","MALE","m":

to

case "Male\n","M\n","MALE\n","m\n":

And there was another error that might have been found by having people try entering their gender. A sin of omission.

adding "male\n" should be added as a possibility

gives us

case "Male\n","M\n","MALE\n","m\n","male\n":

And the program will identify me as male if I enter any of the male replies.

```
    case "Male\n","M\n","MALE\n","m\n":

  //spelling counts so try for all possibilities


      print( "Thank you sir!")
   default:  //if you are not male…
      print( "Thank you ma'am'!")

  }
```

```
Please enter your gender
Male
Thank you sir!
Program ended with exit c
```

(Figure 12.9 Taking care of the "\n" fixes the error.)

The nil coalescing operator will never have to give the error substitute. as "\n" would not be considered to be nil. But as you create projects with text fields having an empty box failsafe may save you from crashes.

Understanding Swift

thirteen

Enumerations an Intro

Enumerations are not quite what they were in C an C++. In some ways I liked C and C++ enumerations as they were.

I could use a C enum Numbers to declare all-cap words for the numbers from ZERO to TEN. It would be the same as using a #define Zero 0, or const int TEN = 10;

```
//  Created by David Curran on 12/8/15.
//  Copyright © 2015 David Francis Curran. All rights reserved.
//

#include <stdio.h>

int main(int argc, const char * argv[]) {


    enum Numbers {

        ZERO, ONE, TWO, THREE, FOUR, FIVE, SIX, SEVEN, EIGHT, NINE, TEN

    };


    enum Numbers nowTime = THREE;

    printf("\nnowTime is == %d and THREE is == %d\n", nowTime,THREE);

    nowTime = TEN;

    printf("\nnowTime is == %d and TEN is == %d\n", nowTime,TEN);

    nowTime = 15;
```

```
printf("\nnowTime is == %d and 15 is == %d\n", nowTime,15);


    return 0;


}
```

Note the line "enum Numbers nowTime = THREE;" The word "enum" is essential. You cannot use simply write "Numbers nowTime = THREE;" You will get

Understanding Swift

```c
//   main.c
//   EnumTests
//
//   Created by David Curran on 12/8/15.
//   Copyright © 2015 David Francis Curran. All rights rese
//

#include <stdio.h>

int main(int argc, const char * argv[]) {

    enum Numbers {

        ZERO, ONE, TWO, THREE, FOUR, FIVE, SIX, SEVEN, EIC

    };

    enum Numbers nowTime = THREE;

    printf("\nnowTime is == %d and THREE is == %d\n", nowT

    nowTime = TEN;

    printf("\nnowTime is == %d and TEN is == %d\n", nowTim

    nowTime = 15;

    printf("\nnowTime is == %d and 15 is == %d\n", nowTime

    return 0;
}
```

```
nowTime is == 3 and '

nowTime is == 10 and

nowTime is == 15 and
Program ended with e:
```

(Figure 13.1 An enum set up in C.)

I wish Apple had kept the old and called the new kind of enumerations something else. But...

Apple recommends that you start an new Enumeration type with a capital letter and do not make them plural.

That is: enum "Number" rather than enum "numbers". (You don't always have to agree with Apple's suggestions. I call my old enum Numbers because that is what they are.)

In C and C++ Numbers is not a type. You have to write
"enum Numbers" nowTime = THREE; You cannot use "Numbers" By itself.

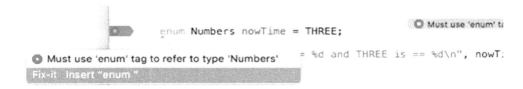

(Figure 13.2 In C something declared as an enum is not a type. So in C and C++ the word "enum" needs to be included.)

Apple did have some good reasons for making the rules concerning their new enum, however. The new enum has many more capabilities than the old C enum. And since the old C enum had values that could only be ints, type safety was not an issue. But Apple's new enum does not have to be only an Int in Swift.

Since you are likely asking yourself how is this enum different than the old. Let's see what we have to do to make our Swift enum as much like the old as possible.
Create a new playground for enums. And enter:

```
enum Numbers {  //Note word case before each value. This can be done differently but
without case you cannot have a rawValue—a value of some consistent type.


    case ZERO
    case ONE
    case TWO
    case THREE
    case FOUR
    case FIVE
    case SIX
    case SEVEN
    case EIGHT
    case NINE
    case TEN


}  //no need for a ;
```

This sets up an enum named Numbers but it has no values. Apple likes to call them rawValues.

Very simply rawValues are values given to a enum.

In Swift "Numbers" is now a type and trying to write

enum Numbers as you do in C or C++ will lead to an error.

An explicit cast will work but it is not written as it would be in C or C++.

var count: ~~enum~~ Numbers = .EIGHT //will give you a ERROR

var count1: Numbers = .EIGHT //will work.

an implicit cast will also work.

var **count** = Numbers.EIGHT

Note that to set a variable or constant to one of the values in our Numbers, you use a period before the value. As in .EIGHT above.

But our enum Numbers will not have any values showing in your playground.

```
//: Playground - noun: a place where people can play

import Cocoa

enum Numbers {  //Note word case before each value.

    case ZERO
    case ONE
    case TWO
    case THREE
    case FOUR
    case FIVE
    case SIX
    case SEVEN
    case EIGHT
    case NINE
    case TEN

}   //no need for a ;

//To access a value in our enum use a period before the name

var count1: Numbers = .EIGHT //will work. This explicitly casts     EIGHT
count1 to a Numbers value

//an implicit cast will also work.

var count = Numbers.EIGHT  //this implicitly casts count to        EIGHT
                    a Numbers value
```

(Figure 13.3 In Swift values for the enum do not show in the playground until you use them as in count and count1 above.)

As you can see only EIGHT shows in the gutter. Add a print(count1) if you like!

The enum above does not have any base or raw values. An enum in swift doesn't actually need base values to be effective. Take this enum for instance.

```swift
enum PlantsNameHint {

    case my, very, eager
    case mother, just, served, up
    case nine, pies

}

var aPlanet = PlantsNameHint.served

switch(aPlanet){

case .my:

    print( "Mercury" )

case .very:

    print( "Venus" )

case .eager:

    print( "Earth" )

case .mother:

    print( "Mars" )

case .just:

    print( "Jupiter" )
```

```
case .served:

    print( "Saturn" )

case .up:

    print( "Uranus" )

case .nine:

    print( "Neptune" )

case .pies:

    print( "Poor Pluto" )


}
```

//Prints "Saturn"

But lets say your goal for the moment is the make this like the C or C++ enum. Actually this is not that hard. Let us redo our Numbers enum.

```
enum Numbers:Int {
```

Will actually change the enum from an unspecified type to type Int. It will also give each case item an Int value starting with zero.

If you change your enum Numbers to include :Int it will not look any different than the figure above, except for the inclusion of :Int.

Playgrounds have Ghosts

When you create a project in Xcode in C or C++ or Object-C or Swift the project menu has in addition to RUN, BUILD, etc. a CLEAN choice. This is because sometime our projects remember things they should not, and we need to rebuild from scratch. CLEAN deletes the current build and starts from scratch. Playgrounds sometimes remember things, I'll call them ghosts, that are no longer there. I mention this because you might find one working on this section.

Now we will change enum Numbers to enum Numbers:Int and make a few changes. We will by adding the :Int giving our enum what is referred to as a rawValue. This used to be referred to as toRaw() but that no longer works in the current version of Swift. If you try to access a rawValue without specifying what type your enum is you will get an error.

Note that we can begin the number of this enum with any int value we want. The default is 0. If you have any problems with the code below change

case ZERO

to

case ZERO = 0

Enter this into your playground:

enum **Numbers**:Int { //Note word case before each value.

    case ZERO
    case ONE

```
    case TWO
    case THREE
    case FOUR
    case FIVE
    case SIX
    case SEVEN
    case EIGHT
    case NINE
    case TEN


}  //no need for a ;

var time:Numbers = .FIVE

if time == .FIVE {

    print(time.rawValue)


    let theTime = time.rawValue
    print(theTime)
    print(theTime)
}
```

```
enum Numbers:Int {  //Note word case before each value.

    case ZERO
    case ONE
    case TWO
    case THREE
    case FOUR
    case FIVE
    case SIX
    case SEVEN
    case EIGHT
    case NINE
    case TEN

}   //no need for a ;

var time:Numbers = .FIVE                          FIVE

if time == .FIVE {

    print(time.rawValue)                          "5\n"


    let theTime = time.rawValue                   5
    print(time.rawValue)                          "5\n"
    print(theTime)                                "5\n"
```

```
5
5
5
```

(Figure 13.4 In Swift the default for numbering is 0 for, in this case, ZERO.)

Note that is the above case "theTime" is a constant Int which equals 5. It is not an instance of
the enum Numbers.

In the above example case is on every line, but you do not have to use the word case for each new value in your enum. The code below:

```
enum YourInt: Int {

    case a,b,c

}
```

works the same as with only the name of the enum different.

```
enum MyInt: Int {
        case a
        case b
        case c

}
```

You do need to use the word case at least once to get rawValue.

```
enum errorNum {

        a, b, c

}
```

```
enum errorNum {

        a, b, c

}
```

(Figure 13.5 The word case is missing.)

var **myBubble** = MyInt.c
var **yourBubble** = YourInt.c

print(**myBubble**.rawValue)
print(**yourBubble**.rawValue)

```
import Cocoa

enum YourInt: Int {

    case a,b,c

}

enum MyInt: Int {

    case a
    case b
    case c

}

var myBubble = MyInt.c              c
var yourBubble = YourInt.c          c

print( myBubble.rawValue)           "2\n"
print( yourBubble.rawValue)         "2\n"
```

(Figure 13.6 No difference in using case a, b, c or case a<newline> case b<newline> case 3.)

Note there is no difference based on having all our enum members being declared on the same line as case or on individual lines with case. UNLIKE SWITCHES where all values on the same line after case are treated as if they are the same value.

Understanding Swift

There was a ~~fromRaw()~~ in Swift but that had been replaced (As Apple puts it) by:

There are shades of Apple's Obj-C in that statement. What it means is if you want to stick a raw value from our MyInt enum into myBubble using a raw value you have to do it like this.

myBubble = MyInt(rawValue: 0)!

print(myBubble)

print(myBubble.rawValue)

```
myBubble = MyInt( rawValue: 0)!        a

print(myBubble)                        "a\n"

print(myBubble.rawValue)               "0\n"
```

(Figure 13.7 Use the init?(rawValue:) initializer to make an instance of an enumeration from a raw value.)

Even if we change to a new variable the rawValue: MUST be a member of our MyInt enum.

That is

var myNewBubble = MyInt(rawValue: 3) WARNING! Tries to access a value of MyInt 3 that does not exist in MyInt. So the value transferred to myNewBubble will be nil.

```
var myNewBubble = MyInt( rawValue: 3)        nil
```

(Figure 13.8 myNewBubble == nil IT DOES NOT EXIST.)

Entering

myNewBubble!.rawValue //here will cause an error!

Entering

myNewBubble = .b   // you will see b in your gutter.

is valid. myNewBubble was set up as an instance of MyInt and can now be assigned to valid MyInt values. But myNewBubble, because it was originally set to nil is an optional. And it MUST be unwrapped to access its rawValue.

```
var myNewBubble = MyInt( rawValue: 3)      nil

print(myNewBubble)                         "nil\n"

myNewBubble = .b                           b

myNewBubble!.rawValue                      1
```

(Figure 13.9 myNewBubble must be unwrapped: myNewBubble!)

What will happen if you type in:

var myEvenNewerBubble = MyInt.c
myEvenNewerBubble = MyInt(rawValue:0)
print (myEvenNewerBubble)

```
var myEvenNewerBubble = MyInt.c                                        c
myEvenNewerBubble = MyInt(rawValue:0)    ◎ Value of optional type 'MyInt?'    a
print (myEvenNewerBubble)|              not unwrapped; did you mean to use '!' or '?'?   a\n
◎ Value of optional type 'MyInt?' not unwrapped; did you mean to use '!' or '?'?
Fix-it  Insert "!"
```

(Figure 13.10 Swift and Xcode will tell you if you need to unwrap.)

You will get an error asking you to unwrap MyInt(rawValue:0)

Fixing it will add a !

Lets go back and look at:

var myNewBubble = MyInt(rawValue: 3)

again. This does NOT need a ! to unwrap it. As its value is nil and unwrapping it would create an error.

```
●    var myNextBubble = MyInt( rawValue: 3)!              ● error
     ● Execution was interrupted, reason: EXC_BAD_INSTRUCTION
                (code=EXC_I386_INVOP, subcode=0x0).
```

(Figure 13.11 There is no 3 so unwrapping it causes an error.)

Next we will try

var myNextNewBubble = MyInt(rawValue: nil) //Fails saying the expected value after rawValue has to be an Int.

So keep in mind with an enum like

```
enum MyInt2: Int {

    case a, b, c

}
```

that if you use Use the init?(rawValue:)

var someVariable = Name_Of_Enum(rawValue:
Some_Int_Not_Included_In_"Name_Of_Enum")(! not needed or Wanted)

someVariable = .SOME_VALID_MEMBER_OF_ENUM

someVariable(! needed).rawValue

var myNextNewBubble = MyInt2(rawValue:33) //33 is way off
myNextNewBubble = .a
myNextNewBubble!.rawValue

And if you use

var someOtherVariable = Name_Of_Enum(rawValue:
Some_Int_Included_In_Name_Of_Enum)(! needed)

someOtherVariable = .SOME_VALID_MEMBER_OF_ENUM

someOtherVariable(! not needed or Wanted).rawValue

var myEvenNewerBubble = MyInt2.c
myEvenNewerBubble = MyInt2(rawValue:0)!

```
myEvenNewerBubble.rawValue
print (myEvenNewerBubble)
```

You will find if you answer the section questions below that enum SomeFloatEnum: Float {}
is not much different than enum SomeIntEnum: Int{}

But what about Strings? Type in:

```
enum MyStringEnum: String {

    case sweet = "Sweet", young, thing

}

var string1 = MyStringEnum.sweet

string1.rawValue

string1 = .young

string1.rawValue
```

```
enum MyStringEnum: String {

    case sweet = "Sweet", young, thing

}

var string1 = MyStringEnum.sweet

string1.rawValue;

string1 = .young

string1.rawValue;
```

(Figure 13.12 Using rawValue to find the value of an enum.)

Since a String was not provided for young the string "young" was provided for us.

```
enum myCountingString: String {

  case one, two, three

}

var countTwo = myCountingString.two.rawValue

countTwo == "Two"
```

One final note for this section. Keep in mind there is a difference between

```
enum MyIntToo: Int{

    case a, b, c, d
}
```

let ace = MyIntToo.a

let doc = MyIntToo.a.rawValue

here ace == a   which is an instance of MyIntToo

but doc == 0 and is only an Int. There is no doc.a, or doc.b or doc.c or doc.d

That is it for the first section on Enumerations. We will get back to them in book II after covering a few more subjects.   There is a lot more we can do with enumerations.

Questions

1) given

```
enum An_ENUM: Int {

    case a, b, c
}
```

var Y = Int!()

var X = An_ENUM(rawValue: Y)

a. var z = An_ENUM.a

    z will equal 2 (z == 2)

b. var Y = Int!() will cause a fatal error

c. var X An_ENUM(rawValue: Y) will cause a fatal error

d. var X will be nil

2) given

    enum aLittleEnum: Int {

    case a = 15 ,b,c,d,e,f,g

    }

    var w = aLittleEnum.c

    What will

    w.rawValue

    be?

a. 2

b. 3

c. 17

d. 18

3) given

```
enum MyFloatEnum: Float {

 case a, b, c, d, q, e, m
 }

var f = MyFloatEnum.e
```

What will

```
f.rawValue
```

be?

a. nil

b. FATAL ERROR

c. 3.0

d. 5.0

fourteen

Dictionaries

Understanding Swift

When I was working in C or C++ I would sometimes make arrays of arrays

```
int myArrayOfArrays[10][10];
```

or

```
int myArrayOfArraysOfArrays[10][10][10]; //and on and on and on
```

You don't exactly see much of that in Swift.

You could set up an Array of 1000 Int values.

```
var aThousandIntArray = [Int](count: 1000, repeatedValue: 0)
```

And then play with the values in it.

But the point is always to collect data in a way that we need to use that. And Swift does give us the opportunity to collect data in what is know as a dictionary. It is not quite like an `int myArrayOfArrays[10][10];` But you could make something close.

Lets say we make a myArrayOfArrays with 100 values and say myArrayOfArrays[0][0] = 5; myArrayOfArrays[0][1] = 7; myArrayOfArrays[0][2] = 9;

all the way to myArrayOfArrays[10][10] = 122;

```
var A_DICTIONARY_NAME:[Int : Int] = [ 0 : 5, 1: 7, 2 : 9]
```

Instead Swift has the dictionary.

Each dictionary entry is composed of two items, the first being the key and the second the value. Here is a dictionary with strings for both the key and the value.

var **myExampleDictionary:** [String : String] = ["Key" : "Value"]

Items in a Dictionary are sorted by their key in a hash table which the user never sees. Swift takes care of the sorting behind the scenes. Very simply Swift takes your Key, breaks it down into a sortable code and finds your Key when you need it. Keys can be any type, Int, Double, String, that can be converted to a hash number for storage. And values can be of any type.

A Dictionary can be created explicitly.

var or let dictionaryName(colon:) [type name for key (colon:) type name for value] = [key of specified type (colon:) value of specified type (**comma separator if needed**) .... key of specified type (colon:) value of specified type]

You could use a dictionary for a collection of last and first names, with the names sorted by surname.

var **myDictionary:**[String : String] = ["LastNameOne":"David", "LastNameTwo": "Paul", "LastNameThree":"Pat", "LastNameFour":"Sean"]

//This could also be written as:

var **myDictionary2:** Dictionary<String , String> = ["LastNameOne":"David", "LastNameTwo": "Lee", "LastNameThree":"Pat", "LastNameFour":"Sean"]

or you can declare you dictionary inexplicitly if you make sure there is no confusion as to what it is you are inexplicitly declaring.

var **myDictionary3** = ["LastNameOne":"David", "LastNameTwo": "Lee", "LastNameThree":"Pat", "LastNameFour":"Sean"]

Understanding Swift

There can be no doubt in the above that both dictionary types are Strings. But if I type in some items with values that may be Ints and end up Doubles look at how the order changes in the gutter.

var myFunFile = ["Dave": 11,"Pat" :12, "Sean" : 14.01]

```
var myDictionary3  =       ["LastNameOne": "David", "LastNameTwo": "Lee",
                            "LastNameThree": Pat, "LastNameFour": Sean]
    ["LastNameOne":"Dav
    id", "LastNameTwo":
    "Lee",
    "LastNameThree":"Pa
    t",
    "LastNameFour":"Sea
    n"]

var myFunFile =          ["Sean": 14.01, Dave : 11, Pat : 12]
    ["Dave": 11,"Pat" :
    12, "Sean" : 14.01]
```

(Figure 14.1 You may be surprised at how Swift orders items you entered.)

Swift is recognizing these as doubles because of the one double value. Sean is first because of Swift hash table sort which is behind the scenes.

You can check that swift has designated the values as Doubles with a for-in loop

var myFunFile = ["Dave": 11,"Pat" :12, "Sean" : 14.01]

for (key, value) in myFunFile{

  print("\(value * 0.202)")

}

prints out:

2.83002

2.222

2.424

If you were to change the 14.01 value for Sean to 14 (an Int) the code above will cause an error when you try to multiple that Int by the double 0.202.

To retrieve one value one value from a dictionary we can use

```
let myNameNumber = myFunFile["Pat"]
```

```
//Will give us the value associated with ["Pat"] which is 12.
```

```
print( myNameNumber! * 0.202)  //We need the ! as myNameNumber is an optional
```

We get:

12

"2.424\n"

Lets go back to trying to build something like my myArrayOfArrays[10][10] in C or C++. We will call the dictionary myDictionaryTenTen.

We could do this to fill the entire myDictionaryTenTen with numbers.

First we'll declare the dictionary giving it some initial values.

```
var myDictionaryTenTen:[Int : Int] = [ 0 : 5, 1 : 7, 2 : 9]
```

Then fill the rest of our hundred slots with the help of a for loop.

```
for var i = 3; i < 100; i++ {
```

myDictionaryTenTen[i] = (i + (i % 10) * 2) + 5

}

To get the entire dictionary

print(myDictionaryTenTen)

We can assess values with something like this. For item 99.

var **myresulting** = myDictionaryTenTen[99]

print 122 in the gutter.

Or for just getting item 9 in the gutter

myDictionaryTenTen[9]

prints 32 in the gutter.

```
var myDictionaryTenTen:[Int : Int] = [ 0 : 5,        [2: 9, 0: 5,
    1 : 7, 2 : 9]

for var i = 3; i < 100; i++ {

    myDictionaryTenTen[i] = (i + (i % 10) * 2) +      (97 times)
       5

}

print( myDictionaryTenTen)                            "[17: 36, 14

var myresulting = myDictionaryTenTen[99]             122
myDictionaryTenTen[9]                                 32
```

```
[17: 36, 14: 27, 30: 35, 77: 96, 68: 89, 99: 122, 3: 14, 32: 41
28: 49, 84: 97, 6: 23, 50: 55, 12: 21, 23: 34, 25: 40, 90: 95,
99, 45: 60, 63: 74, 11: 18, 37: 56, 2: 9, 98: 119, 27: 46, 71:
87: 106, 76: 93, 21: 28, 9: 32, 44: 57, 35: 50, 15: 30, 29: 52,
85: 100, 56: 73, 97: 116, 89: 112, 22: 31, 18: 39, 53: 64, 62:
57: 76, 69: 92, 91: 98, 41: 48, 93: 104, 20: 25, 49: 72, 38: 59
42: 51, 47: 66, 59: 82, 39: 62, 34: 47, 46: 63, 67: 86, 95: 110
96: 113, 7: 26, 43: 54, 16: 33, 51: 58, 64: 77, 31: 38, 26: 43,
66: 83, 73: 84, 8: 29, 79: 102, 65: 80, 40: 45, 24: 37, 83: 94,
13: 24, 72: 81, 70: 75, 19: 42, 88: 109, 60: 65, 86: 103, 1: 7,
10: 15, 75: 90, 55: 70, 48: 69, 33: 44, 54: 67, 94: 107, 4: 17,
```

(Figure 14.2 Printing out specific key values. Note how the 100 are ordered in a print().)

We can change the value of our values in our dictionary if we know the key.

If you look at Apples own book on Swift you'll see this

updateValue(_: forKey:)

as the function to use for updating a value you know the key for. There is a bit of their old object-C here. This actually translates to:

myDictionaryTenTen.updateValue(33, forKey: 9)

updateValue(has to be attached to your dictionary's name)

_: actually means put in the value followed by a comma, followed by the instruction word with colon forKey: followed by the key and then a closing)

myDictionaryTenTen[9]

and the result in the gutter will be

33

I think I'll leave our comparison to myArrayOfArrays[10][10] here. Because though our myDictionaryTenTen has similar values so far, it can easily be changed. Suppose I want to add another value.

Lets pick a key we haven't used: 199.

In an array there would be 99 missing values. But a dictionary is not an array.

so

myDictionaryTenTen[199] = (199 + (199 % 10) * 2) + 5

Just adds to value 222 to a dictionary with one hundred and one items.

We have been adding values to this myDictionaryTenTen dictionary and using what appear to be ints as the keys.

myDictionaryTenTen.count //gives us 101`

We have used 99 as a key in this dictionary so what will 099 give us.

myDictionaryTenTen[099] = (099 + (099 % 10) * 2) + 5

gives us the same value 122 as myDictionaryTenTen[99] **and**

myDictionaryTenTen.count //still equals 101

as does

myDictionaryTenTen[3*33] = (3*33 + (3*33 % 10) * 2) + 5

also gives us a count of 101. The keys are evaluated as per their declaration, in this case and Int.

Removing A Value

Apple gives us removeValueForKey(_:) as the way to remove something.

Again we have to attach this to our dictionary's name and put in only the key.

myDictionaryTenTen.count

myDictionaryTenTen[100]

myDictionaryTenTen[199]

myDictionaryTenTen.count

myDictionaryTenTen.removeValueForKey(199)

myDictionaryTenTen[199]

myDictionaryTenTen.count

myDictionaryTenTen.count	101
myDictionaryTenTen[100]	nil
myDictionaryTenTen[199]	222
myDictionaryTenTen.count	101
myDictionaryTenTen.removeValueForKey(199)	222
myDictionaryTenTen[199]	nil
myDictionaryTenTen.count	100

(Figure 14.3 Showing results for using .count and ,removeValueForKey())

Note that although there are 101 items in our dictionary the key 100 is shown as nil. After the value for key 199 is removed that too is shown as nil.

Also note that myDictionaryTenTen.removeValueForKey(199) gives us the value removed:

222

Understanding Swift

As we learned in our For-In-Loop we can use the For-In-Loop to go through our dictionary. For fun lets put our value for key 199 back

```
myDictionaryTenTen[199] = 1000

for( whoCaresWhatICallTheKey, whoCaresWhatICallTheValue) in myDictionaryTenTen {

        print( "\(whoCaresWhatICallTheKey):\(whoCaresWhatICallTheValue)")
}
```

Try it in your playground!

Lets try something new type into your playground.

```
print(myDictionaryTenTen.keys)
print(myDictionaryTenTen.values)
```

Not to impressive yet? Well you wouldn't use
.keys
or
.values in that way. What you might do is something like this.

```
for SomeSillyValue in myDictionaryTenTen.values {

  if SomeSillyValue % 11 == 0 {

      print("SomeSillyValue) "
}
```

And We Get:

55

99

33

66

110

88

33

77

44

What .keys and .values tells Swift is to single out either keys or values.

fifteen

Working With Strings

Understanding Swift

Strings are a little different in Swift. In C and C++ strings were char arrays filed with characters.

instead of

char aLetter = 'a';

We have

var aLetter = "o";

var anotherletter: Character = "k"

note we use double quotes [NEVER SMART QUOTES] for Characters. For now, just keep Characters in mind.

How do we know that these are indeed Characters and not Strings?

We can add Strings together in Swift but we adding Characters is a bit more complex.

var word = aLetter + anotherLetter

```
var aLetter = "o";

var anotherLetter: Character = "k"

var word = aLetter + anotherLetter
```

```
Playground execution failed: /var/folders/2j/pk_382yd4td69_gb3sk65wdr0000gn/T/.
playground673.swift:12:20: error: binary operator '+' cannot be applied to oper
and 'Character'
var word = aLetter + anotherLetter
            ------- ^ --------------
/var/folders/2j/pk_382yd4td69_gb3sk65wdr0000gn/T/./lldb/1358/playground673.swif
an argument list of type '(String, String)'
var word = aLetter + anotherLetter
                             ^
```

(Figure 15.1 Characters in Swift cannot be SIMPLY added together to form Strings.)

So the above gives us an error message. We cannot just add Characters. We will see later we can append a Character to a word but that takes a little care.

Is there such a thing as an implicit Character?

var myWord1 = "n"

var myWord2 = "o"

var myFinalWord = myWord1 + myWord2

```
var myWord1 = "n"                                      "n"
var myWord2 = "o"                                      "o"
var myFinalWord = myWord1 + myWord2                    "no"
```

(Figure 15.2 If you can add two single character variables or constants together they are Strings not Characters.)

As you can see Swift interpreted myWord1 and myWord2 as Strings and not Characters.

Characters like Floats have to be explicitly declared.

So my first question when I looked at Strings in Swift was how do I access the individual Characters? Let's try to access a character in our "Hello, playground" str.

var aThirdLetter: Character = str[0] //crashes

```
○   var aThirdLetter: Character = str[0]

    ▶

Playground execution failed: /var/folders/2i/pk 382vd4td69 ab3:
/./lldb/564/playground143.swift:15:31: error: 'subscript' is
unavailable: cannot subscript String with an Int, see the
documentation comment for discussion
    var aThirdLetter: Character = str[0]
                                  ^
Swift.String:3:12: note: 'subscript' has been explicitly marked
unavailable here
        public subscript (i: Int) -> Character { get }
```

(Figure 15.3 You cannot set a value for a Character by pointing to a location in a String using Ints.)

How do we get ahold of the individual characters in a Sting like str that Swift gave us when we opened the playground. i.e. var str = "Hello, playground"

This used to work but no longer:

```
var theLetter: Character = "o"

for aCharacter in str{

    if aCharacter == theLetter{

        print(theLetter)
    }
}
```

```
Playground execution failed: /var/folders/2j/pk_382yd4td69_gb3sk65wdr000
playground29.swift:177:19: error: value of type 'String' has no member '
for aCharacter in str{
                  ^--
```

(Figure 15.4 This no longer works as is.)

Now one way to do this is to append .characters at the end of our String.

```
for myCharacter in str.characters{
    print (myCharacter)
}
//results in


H
e
l
l
o
,
```

p
l
a
y
g
r
o
u
n
d

Another slightly different way to do the same thing is:

```
for index in str.characters.indices {

  print("\(str[index])")

}
```

Try the above and see if it give you the same results. In the first we access the characters directly. In the second we get the index of each character and then find it in the string using str[index]. The important thing to remember is the index is not equivalent to an Int.

var myOtherCharacter = ["D,A,V,E"]//declares an array of Strings with one String so far. and gives us:

["D,A,V,E"] in the gutter

print(myOtherCharacter[0]) //gives us "D,A,V,E"

Understanding Swift

To make an array of Characters we must declare it explicitly with Character in []

var **myCharacter**: [Character] = ["D","A","V","E"]

//We can convert this array of Character(s) to a string

explicitly

var **myString**: String = String(myCharacter)

or implicitly

var **myString** = String(myCharacter)

Which will give us "DAVE\n" //note that using String() adds a "\n"
And DAVE in the output.

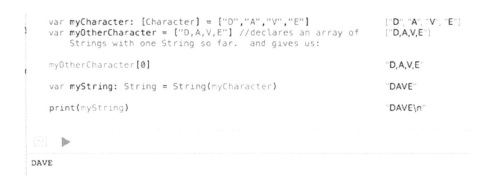

```
var myCharacter: [Character] = ["D","A","V","E"]          ["D", "A", "V", "E"]
var myOtherCharacter = ["D,A,V,E"] //declares an array of   ["D,A,V,E"]
    Strings with one String so far.  and gives us:

myOtherCharacter[0]                                       "D,A,V,E"

var myString: String = String(myCharacter)               "DAVE"

print(myString)                                          "DAVE\n"
```

DAVE

(Figure 15.5 An array of Characters. A string with commas. Proving we have an array of Strings. Converting an array of Characters to a String. Printing the String.)

Is the "\n" included in myString? We can use the familiar count with characters this way.

myString.**characters.count** //and we get 4 so No the "\n" is not included in the count of characters as there are only 4. And since the index starts at 0 the "\n" is at position 4.

[0][1][2][3][4]

[D][A][V][E][\n] //count gives us the count of characters and there are only 4.

We can add a character to our myString with .append(a character) Let's imagine we are calling out to Dave.

however:

myString.**append**("?") //fails because the "?" could be interpreted as a String. And Swift finds this ambiguous. One way we can add a single character is:

var **myQuestionMark**: Character = "?"
myString.**append(myQuestionMark)**

gives us "Dave?"

Although you can't simply add a character to a string

var **newWord** = myString + myQuestionMark //fails

var **newWord1** = myString += myQuestionMark // fails

Type in the line

        var **myString2**: String = String(myCharacter)

and command click on the word String.

In the list of options String has one of the first things listed is:

 public var **startIndex:** Index { **get** }

Strings in Swift are not like our C or C++ arrays of letters in the the index is not just a list of ints. But there is an index and Swift does give us ways to access them;

if we write

myString.startIndex //we get 0 in the gutter. But that 0 is not readily available as an ordinary int with value 0.

To get the first character in our String myString we need to write.

myString[myString.startIndex] **// which uses** myString.startIndex as the index and gives us "D"

As you'll notice there are other ways to access the private index of a String.

myString.endIndex //gives us 5. Which is the same as

myString.characters.count

```
myString.endIndex //gives us 5. Which is the    5
    same as
myString.characters.count;                      5
```

(Figure 15.6 endIndex is the same as .characters.count)

But we know from C and C++ that DAVE last index only contains 0, 1, 2, 3 and 4. The \n

that you see in the gutter is not considered part of the string. Think of the \n as more of a

reminder that print() will always give a a return at the end of the line.

print(myString[myString.endIndex]) //results in a crash because as in C and C++ it is like

saying for

```
char name[] = "Dave";
printf("%c",name[5]);
```

```
char name[] = "Dave";
printf("%c",name[5]);                    Array index 5 is p
                                         the array (which conta
```

(Figure 15.7 Going past the end of an array of chars is dangerous in C.)

So

myString[myString.endIndex] //will give us an error.

How do we move through the string? Swift provides a few ways:

myString.endIndex.predecessor() //this provides us not with what we'd expect but the index
of endIndex.

myString[myString.endIndex.predecessor()] //this gives us the Character at the predecessor()
position that is the index before endIndex. This is what we want.

endIndex is always past the end of our String!

Using Predecessor takes us one step back. And give us a "?"

Adding additional .predecessor()s will take us further back.

myString[myString.endIndex.predecessor().predecessor()] //takes us two steps back and gives us an "E"

And

myString[myString.endIndex.predecessor().predecessor().predecessor().predecessor().predecessor()]

will take us all the way back to "D"

But that is a pretty clunky way to get around. And if we add one too many

.predecessor()

we'll get a fatal error.

So Swift also gives us.

.successor()

myString.startIndex.successor() //works much like .predecessor except successor() moves forward.

```
myString.startIndex.successor()                        1

myString.startIndex.successor().successor()            2

myString[myString.startIndex.successor()]             'A'

myString[myString.startIndex.successor().            'V'
    successor()]   //gives us "V"
```

(Figure 15.8 Moving around using .startIndex.successor() and adding additional .successor()s.)

Do not access a Character for an index that does not exist.

myString.endIndex.predecessor().successor() // is 5 which as you've seen does not exist and trying to access a Character there will lead to an error.

Do not access an index which does not exist.

myString.startIndex.predecessor()

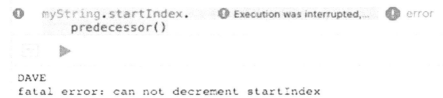

(Figure 15.9 However just as in C and C++ you cannot go to nonexistent locations. .startIndex.predecessor() fails.)

.advanceBy() actually takes an int as an argument. It needs something like startIndex as a starting position.

myString.startIndex.advancedBy(2) //gives us 2

myString[myString.startIndex.advancedBy(2)] //gives us "V"

Going as high as myString.characters.count or its equivalent myString.endIndex in advancedBy() will cause a error.

advancedBy() presents us with another way to print out the characters in a String. Try this in your playground.

```
var counter = 0 //counter must be set to an int not an index

while counter < str.characters.count { // str.characters.count does return an Int.

    print(str[str.startIndex.advancedBy(counter)]) //advanced by takes the Int argument.

    counter++
}
```

.advancedBy(Int) can take negative values. Try this in your playground with our Swift startup String str.

```
var countOfCharacters = str.characters.count // str.characters.count returns an int

str.endIndex //remember we can't use this it is an index not an int.

var counterNeg = countOfCharacters

str.endIndex.advancedBy( -counterNeg)

while counterNeg > 0 {
```

```
print( str[str.endIndex.advancedBy( -counterNeg)] )
    counterNeg--
}
```

Consider, .endIndex does not contain a character but it is a valid next index and a character can be inserted there.

```
myString.insert("!", atIndex: myString.endIndex)  //doesn't overwrite but inserts at the
endIndex of the string.
```

but .endIndex is not a valid place to remove a character as there is no character there. The character we just inserted, "!" is not one removed from the end so it is at

```
myString.endIndex.predecessor()
```

To remove the character ahead of it, the original "?" we do this.

```
myString.removeAtIndex(myString.endIndex.predecessor().predecessor()) //removes the "?"
we pushed forward.
```

```
print(myString)
```

Understanding Swift

```
myString.insert("!", atIndex: myString.endIndex)  //dc
    overwrite but inserts at the endIndex of the strir

myString.removeAtIndex(myString.endIndex.predecessor()
    predecessor()) //removes the "?" we pushed forwarc

print(myString)
```

(Figure 15.10 Using .insert and .removeAtIndex to change a String. Note that String indices are not Ints.)

There is even a .removeRange(_:) method for our String.

Note that when Apple indicates something by _: that value is just inserted without any other instruction.

var **aRange** = str.startIndex.advancedBy(7)...str.startIndex.advancedBy(10)

//lets add some needed punctuation.

str.insert(".", **atIndex:** str.endIndex)

//What did the parachutist whose chute did not open say?

str.**removeRange**(aRange)

sixteen

String Extras

Unicode scalars are considered words and can be simply added on

for example the code for a skill and crossbones is "\u{2620}"

type in:

var **myFavoriteFlag** = "My favorite flag is "

myFavoriteFlag += "\u{2620}"

print(myFavoriteFlag)

```
var myFavoriteFlag = "My favorite flag is     "My favorite flag is "
myFavoriteFlag += "\u{2620}"                  "My favorite flag is ☠ "
print(myFavoriteFlag)                         "My favorite flag is ☠ \n"
```

```
My favorite flag is ☠
```

(Figure 16.1 Even though the jolly roger is a character as it is added here it is a word.)

We can find a String within our Strings. Lets try with myString (DAVE!)

myString.containsString("AV") //**gives us** true

hasPrefix and hasSuffix are similar

```swift
myString.hasPrefix("DA") //gives true  this is the prefix
myString.hasSuffix("VE") //gives false  this is not the suffix
myString.hasSuffix("E!") //gives true   this is the suffix.

print( "myString has \(myString.characters.count) characters.")

//gives us "myString has 5 characters.\n"

myString.isEmpty //will give us false as there are characters there.

var aBlankString = "" //set this to a blank string

var anotherBlankSting = String() //set this to a blank string

aBlankString.isEmpty    //gives us true
anotherBlankSting.isEmpty //gives us true

aBlankString = myString

if( aBlankString == myString){

    print("These two Strings are equal")

} else {

    print("\u{2620}")

}
```

```
var myString = "PROGRAMMER"                                        "PRO(

myString.hasPrefix("PR")  //gives true   this is the prefix        true
myString.hasSuffix("OG") //gives false   this is not the           false
    suffix
myString.hasSuffix("ER") //gives true    this is the suffix.       true

print( "myString has \(myString.characters.count)                  "mySt
    characters.")

//gives us "myString has 10 characters.\n"

myString.isEmpty //will give us false as there are characters      false
    there.

var aBlankString = ""   //set this to a blank string               ""

var anotherBlankSting = String() //set this to a blank string      ""

aBlankString.isEmpty     //gives us true                           true
anotherBlankSting.isEmpty //gives us true                          true

aBlankString = myString                                            "PRO(

if( aBlankString == myString){

    print("These two Strings are equal")                           "Thes

} else {

    print("\u{2620}")

}
```

(Figure 16.2 hasPrefix, hasSuffix, isEmpty and comparing Strings is all part of Swift.)

seventeen

Working with Structs

Understanding Swift

Structs are much like they are in C and C++ with the exception that structs can have methods in Swift as well as data. We will talk about adding methods to structs in a later part of the book. For now lets just take a quick look at a simple struct in Swift.

```
struct businessCard {

    var firstName = String?()
    var middleName = String?()
    var surName = String?()
    var age = Int?()
        var isFemale = Bool?()


}
```

This is a struct I intend to use for a simple dictionary using the clients phone number for the key. I have used optionals for the name parameters. Since these have yet to be filled in.

Lets imagine we get the idea to set up a bunch of blank cards. And to find out easily if they have been filled in, we want to set the age to 0. A 0 indicating the card is empty. To add single values to a businessCard with optionals it would have to be done this way.

```
//We card a businessCard to add to our dictionary.

var myCard = businessCard(firstName: nil, middleName: nil, surName: nil, age: 0, isFemale: nil)
```

Phone numbers could be an Int or a String. Lets just use an Int here and set up a businessCard dictionary.

var **myBusinessCardDictionary**:[Int : businessCard] = [0:myCard]

```
var str = "Hello, playground"                                    "Hello, p

struct businessCard {

    var firstName = String?()
    var middleName = String?()
    var surName = String?()
    var age = Int?()
    var isFemale = Bool?()

}

var myCard = businessCard(firstName: nil, middleName: nil,       busines
    surName: nil, age: 0, isFemale: nil)

print(myCard.age)                                                "Option

var myBusinessCardDictionary:[Int : businessCard] = [0:myCard]   [0: [nil,
```

```
Optional(0)
```

(Figure 17.1 Creating struct businessCard initializing with optionals.)

First off to make this work for us we'll have to remove the 0 key. The keys are addresses of
sorts. Since there is nothing there we need to delete both key and any value.

myBusinessCardDictionary.removeValueForKey(0)

This gives us an empty dictionary.

Next we'll add data to our mostly empty myCard.

myCard.firstName = "Bob"
myCard.middleName = "David"

```
myCard.surName = "Cats"
myCard.age = 33
myCard.isFemale = false
```

We can add the data to our dictionary in a number of ways. We can use updateValue. Which can also be used to change the values on the card.

```
myBusinessCardDictionary.updateValue(myCard, forKey: 5555551212)
```

or (lets add another value)

```
var myCard2 = businessCard(firstName: "Jan", middleName: "Michelle", surName: "Dogs", age: 32, isFemale: true)
```

Because the keys are the indices of our dictionary we can add the card for Jan above by simply using his phone number as a key.

```
myBusinessCardDictionary[5555551020] = myCard2
```

```
print(myBusinessCardDictionary)
```

Understanding Swift

```
myBusinessCardDictionary.removeValueForKey(0)                  businessCard

//now our dictionary is empty
//print(myBusinessCardDictionary)

//lets add values to our myCard

//We will use a phone number for the key

myBusinessCardDictionary = [5555551212:myCard]                 [5555551212 (nil,nil

//we can fill in our blank card

if myCard.age == 0 {

    myCard.firstName = "Bob"                                   businessCard
    myCard.middleName = "David"                                businessCard
    myCard.surName = "Cats"                                    businessCard
    myCard.age = 33                                            businessCard
    myCard.isFemale = false                                    businessCard

}

//then we can update the value myCard
myBusinessCardDictionary.updateValue(myCard, forKey:           businessCard
    5555551212)

var myCard2 = businessCard(firstName: "Jan", middleName:       businessCard
    "Michelle", surName: "Dogs", age: 32, isFemale: true)

myBusinessCardDictionary[5555551020] = myCard2                 businessCard

//print(myBusinessCardDictionary)

func upDateMyCardAge( myCard: businessCard, NewValueForAge:
    Int)->businessCard{

    var newAgeCard = myCard                                    businessCard

    newAgeCard.age = NewValueForAge                            businessCard


    return newAgeCard                                          businessCard
}

myBusinessCardDictionary.updateValue(upDateMyCardAge( myCard,  businessCard
    NewValueForAge: 27), forKey: 5555551020)

print(myBusinessCardDictionary)                               [5555551212: busine
```

```
Optional(0)
[5555551212: businessCard(firstName: Optional("Bob"), middleName: Optional("David"),
Optional("Cats"), age: Optional(33), isFemale: Optional(false)), 5555551020: busines
Optional("Bob"), middleName: Optional("David"), surName: Optional("Cats"), age: Opti
isFemale: Optional(false))]
```

(Figure 17.2 Changing our businessCardDictionary to include phone numbers as keys first involves deleting the 0 key which includes its data. We can use an age of 0 to tell our program to fill in that card with valid data, and we can add an additional card simply by adding a new card, in this case myCard2.)

eighteen

Functions

I liked C or C++ functions.

```cpp
#include <iostream>

using namespace std;

int giveMeTheAverageMileage( int myMileArray[], int entriesTotal){

    int result = 0;

    for( int x = 0; x < entriesTotal; x++ ){

        result += myMileArray[x];
    }
    return result;
}


int main(int argc, const char * argv[]) {

    int distance[6] = {11,14,56,61,4,2};

    cout << "Average milage == " << giveMeTheAverageMileage(distance, 6) << "\n\n";


}
```

But though I always name my functions and variables so they could be understood and remembered for that they do, Others didn't like people writing functions like this.

```cpp
int doIt( int forbar[], int foo){
```

```
int w = 0;

for( int x = 0; x < foo; x++ ){

    w += forbar[x];
}

return w;
}
```

So Object-C has a lot of instructions written into functions where they have to be and so the function can more easily be understood.

We won't need to use them to translate the above C++ program to Swift:

Create a new playground and call it your functions playground. Type in:

```
var listOfNumbers = [11,14,56,61,4,2]

func giveMeTheAverageMileage(listOfNumbers: Array<Int>) -> Int{

    var total = 0

    for var i = 0; i < listOfNumbers.count; i++ {  //we don't need to know how many items
                                                   //our array has Swift takes care of
that for us.

        total += listOfNumbers[i]
    }
```

return total

}

print(giveMeTheAverageMileage(listOfNumbers))

```
var listOfNumbers = [11,14,56,61,4,2]
func giveMeTheAverageMileage(listOfNumbers: Array<Int>) -> Int{
    var total = 0
        for var i = 0; i < listOfNumbers.count; i++ {

                        //we don't need to know how many ite
                //our array has Swift takes care of that for us

        total += listOfNumbers[i]
    }

    return total

}

print(giveMeTheAverageMileage(listOfNumbers))
```

148

(Figure 18.1 A simple function giving us the average of a group of numbers.)

A model for a function would be

func nameOfFunction(NameOfEntity: type, nameOfNextItemToEnter: type, etc.) -> return type{}

Lets go through these for next example of a function I'll be showing you. It consists of:

Understanding Swift

The word:	func
Name of the function:	returnPrefix
Parameter: type	wordToPrefix:String
.	
.	//as many as you need, separated by commas
.	
Parameter: type	lengthOfPrefixToReturn: Int
An arrow :	->
Return Type: String	

Assignment 1:

Try to write a function based on what you've learned so far that will take a String and a length and return the first length characters in that String. Once you've done yours compare yours with mine below. I'll be using Swift's var **str** = "Hello, playground" as my string.

var **str** = "Hello, playground"

func **returnPrefix**(wordToPrefix:String, **lengthOfPrefixToReturn:** Int) ->String {

  if **lengthOfPrefixToReturn** == 0 {

    return ""
  }

  var **nextIndexMarker** = 1

  //set up an array of Characters

```
var aPrefix:[Character] = [wordToPrefix[wordToPrefix.startIndex]]


lengthOfPrefixToReturn
nextIndexMarker
wordToPrefix.characters.count


while nextIndexMarker < wordToPrefix.characters.count && lengthOfPrefixToReturn >
nextIndexMarker {


aPrefix.append(wordToPrefix[wordToPrefix.startIndex.advancedBy(nextIndexMarker)])

    nextIndexMarker++
  }

  let result:String = String(aPrefix)

  return(result)

}

var myPrefixString = returnPrefix(str,lengthOfPrefixToReturn: 3)

print(myPrefixString)
```

Understanding Swift

```swift
var str = "Hello, playground"

//Here is my function taking a string and returning a prefix of length.

func returnPrefix(wordToPrefix:String, lengthOfPrefixToReturn: Int) ->
    String {

    //check to make sure the length to return is greater than 0

    if lengthOfPrefixToReturn == 0 {

        return ""
    }
    //create a counter of type Int (implicitly)

    var nextIndexMarker = 1


    //set up an array of Characters and initialize it with the first
        Character in our string

    var aPrefix:[Character] = [wordToPrefix[wordToPrefix.startIndex]]

    //the three lines below are only here to show you their values
        before using them
    lengthOfPrefixToReturn
    nextIndexMarker
    wordToPrefix.characters.count


    //we'll use a while loop to add to the Character Array
    while nextIndexMarker < wordToPrefix.characters.count &&
        lengthOfPrefixToReturn > nextIndexMarker {

        aPrefix.append(wordToPrefix[wordToPrefix.startIndex.advancedBy
            (nextIndexMarker)])

        nextIndexMarker++
    }

    // As show previously we can convert an array of Characters into a
        Sting with String()
    //the :String below isn't really necessary

    let result:String = String(aPrefix)

    //as in C and C++ we must furnish a return value
    return(result)

}

//call the function
var myPrefixString = returnPrefix(str,lengthOfPrefixToReturn: 3)

//print our result

print(myPrefixString)
```

(Figure 18.2 returnPrefix() takes a string and a length and returns the prefix of that length.)

Assignment 2:

In our Structs chapter we showed how to use

myBusinessCardDictionary.updateValue(myCard, forKey: 5555551212)

updateValue here requires that an entire myCard by supplied. What if you only wanted to update myCard.age? Say Jan doesn't want to be listed as 30 years old.

Can you write a function that would handle that for you? Try it and compare to my solution below.

```
func upDateMyCardAge( myCard: businessCard, NewValueForAge: Int)->businessCard{

    var newAgeCard = myCard

    newAgeCard.age = NewValueForAge


    return newAgeCard
}
```

myBusinessCardDictionary.updateValue(upDateMyCardAge(myCard, NewValueForAge: 27), forKey: 5555551212)

Understanding Swift

```
struct businessCard {

    var firstName = String?()
    var middleName = String?()
    var surName = String?()
    var age = Int?()
    var isFemale = Bool?()

}

var myCard = businessCard(firstName: "Tom",          business(
    middleName: "NMN", surName: "Swift", age:
    14, isFemale: false)

var myBusinessCardDictionary:[Int :
    businessCard]

myBusinessCardDictionary = [5555551212:myCard]       [5555551

func upDateMyCardAge( myCard: businessCard,
    NewValueForAge: Int)->businessCard{

    var newAgeCard =  myCard                         business(

    newAgeCard.age =   NewValueForAge                business(


    return newAgeCard                                business(
}

myBusinessCardDictionary.updateValue                 business(
    (upDateMyCardAge( myCard, NewValueForAge:
    27), forKey: 5555551212)

//print(myBusinessCardDictionary[0]) //uncomment
    to see error

print(myBusinessCardDictionary[5555551212])            'Optional
```

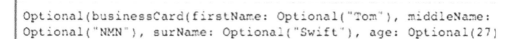

```
Optional(businessCard(firstName: Optional("Tom"), middleName:
Optional("NMN"), surName: Optional("Swift"), age: Optional(27)
```

(Figure 18.3 Writes a function to update one value on our easier businessCard.)

Thank you for reading: We will cover more Swift for C and C++ Programmers in our next book in the series coming out soon.

Assignment 3:

In our chapter on switches we said that if our possible switches were exhaustive as in the true or false example, we did not need a default:

How good is Swift in understanding if a given switch is exhaustive. Lets test it. Write a function whose return value makes the switch exhaustive.

```swift
func SOMEFUNC(anIntValue:Int)->Int{

    //write your code here
}

var valueToSwitchOn =  5

switch(valueToSwitchOn){

case 1:

  print("Opps")

case 2:
```

```
  print("Whoops")

case SOMEFUNC(valueToSwitchOn):

  print("Success if Swift doesn't ask for a default.")

}
```

Can you do it? Try to solve before looking at my solution (if I found one) below.

```
func SOMEFUNC(anIntValue:Int)->Int{

        return(anIntValue)   //returning the value entered should
            always be exhaustive.
}

var valueToSwitchOn =  5

switch(valueToSwitchOn){

case 1:

    print("Opps")

case 2:

    print("Whoops")

case SOMEFUNC(valueToSwitchOn):

    print("Success if Swift doesn't ask for a default.")

 ❶  }
```

```
Playground execution failed: /var/folders/2j/pk_382yd4td69_gb3sk65wd:
1358/playground1877.swift:146:1: error: switch must be exhaustive, co
default clause
}
```

(Figure 18.4 My idea to return the value entered which will always provide a solution did not work. But then you should know if you are a C or C++ programmer, compliers and programmers both are imperfect.)

186

nineteen

Playgrounds

Understanding Swift

```
//: Chapter 3 Playground - noun: a place where people can play

import Cocoa

var str = "Hello, playground"

var bananas = 5

var grapes = 6

print("We have \(grapes) grapes and \(bananas) bananas")

var apples = 4

var oranges = 5

var pears = 6

print("We have \(apples) apples and \(oranges) oranges", terminator: "")
print(" and \(pears) pears")
```

Understanding Swift

//: Chapter 4 Playground - noun: a place where people can play

import Cocoa

var str = "Hello, playground"
var xInt = 1
var yInt = 1

var addition = xInt + yInt

var multiplication = addition * addition

var subtraction = multiplication - yInt

var division = (subtraction * multiplication)/addition

var aDouble = 4.333

var aDoubleToo = 5.999

var modOfTwoDouble = aDoubleToo % aDouble

print(--xInt) //subtracts one before printing
print(yInt--) //subtracts after before print
print(yInt)   //shows the subtracted one

print(++xInt)
print(yInt++)

```
print(yInt)
```

Understanding Swift

```swift
import Cocoa

var str = "Hello, playground"

var x = 5
let myConstX = 5
var z = 5.00
var  y = 5.01
var myDoubleX = 5.00000001



//var mySmallDouble = .69



var mySmallDouble = 0.69




switch(y){

case 5.01:

    var x = 3 //this x is in a different scope than the x above
    print(x)

default:

    print(y)
    print(x)
```

191

```
}

var xTimesMyConstX = x*myConstX

//myConstX = 7  //uncomment to see error

var yTimesZ = z*y

//var MyConstXTimesZ = myConstX*z //uncomment to see error

var  myConstXTimesZInt = myConstX*Int(z)

//25 should appear in the gutter.

var  zTimesMyConstXDouble = Double(myConstX)*z


var  zTimesMyConstXDouble2 = Double(myConstX) * y

var  zTimesMyConstXDouble3 = Double(myConstX) * myDoubleX


let f:Float = 9.99

let d:Double = 9.99

let e = 9.99

var fl = f*1.0002
var dl = d*1.0002
var el = e*1.0002
```

```
let g:Float64 = 9.99

var gl = g*1.0002

let a = Int.max
let b = Int64.max


let aMin = Int.min


let c = Int32.max
let q = Int32.min

let r = UInt32.max

let s = UInt.max
```

Understanding Swift

```swift
import Cocoa

var str = "Hello, playground"

let blue:Bool = true

let red: Int = Int(blue)

print(blue)


print(red)

let one = 1

let boolOne = Bool(one)


let boolSeven = Bool(7)


let notBoolSeven = !boolSeven


var petite = Bool(-1)

var zero = Bool(0)


var big = 100
```

```
var bigCopy = big

var little = 4


var resultOfComparison = big > little   //true
resultOfComparison = big == little              //false
resultOfComparison = little <= big        //true
resultOfComparison = big <= bigCopy             //true
resultOfComparison =  big >= bigCopy  //true
resultOfComparison =  big <= little             //false
```

```
//: Chapter 7 Playground - noun: a place where people can play

import Cocoa

var str = "Hello, playground"

//var dave = '\0'  //uncomment to see error message

//var dave = ['D','a','v','e']  //uncomment to see error message and correction for that error.

var dave = ["D","a","v","e"]

var biElementArray = ["Mom", 7] //this is not an array.  Arrays can ONLY HAVE ONE TYPE
IN THEM. We will discuss what this is when we get to dictionaries.

var aRealArray:[Int] = [5, 7] //this is an array of type Int.

//let anArrayOfInts = [0,1,2,3,4,5,6,7,8,9] //uncomment to see an error not here but below
when we redeclare anArrayOfInts.

//anArrayOfInts[0] = 10 //uncomment to see error. let denotes a constant array the values of
which cannot be changed.

var anArrayOfInts = [0,1,2,3,4,5,6,7,8,9]
anArrayOfInts[0] = 10


print( anArrayOfInts)

anArrayOfInts[0] = 0
//anArrayOfInts[11] = 10  //uncomment to see the error in the output area below.  This goes
beyond the range of the array.
```

anArrayOfInts

print(anArrayOfInts)

anArrayOfInts**.append(**11) //works but don't be confused this is at index 10.

//anArrayOfInts[11] = 5 //would crash as there is no index 11.there is a value of 11 at index 10.

//anArrayOfInts += 12 //uncomment to see why this crashes and gives an error

anArrayOfInts **+=** [12] //works the 12 must be inside []

anArrayOfInts[11] **=** 11 //works because now we've already appended an 11th position. We are just changing the value here.

anArrayOfInts[10] **=** 10

anArrayOfInts **+=** [13] // works and adds a 13th item at the 12th index

anArrayOfInts

var **aStringArray** = ["ma","my","mo"] //Beware of smart quotes!

aStringArray **+=** ["mum"] //works
aStringArray[0] **=** "me" //works

```
var aNewIntArray = [Int]()
var anotherNewIntArray = Array<Int>()
var aNewStringArray = Array<String>()
var anotherNewStringArray = [String]()


aNewIntArray = [0,1,2,3,4,5,6,7,8,9]


aNewIntArray += [10]


aNewStringArray = ["ma","my","mo"]


aNewStringArray += ["mum"]
aNewStringArray[0] = "me" //note the quotes
print(aNewIntArray)


var kot = Array<String>()


kot = ["What","is"]


//By holding the apple command down with your cursor Array you will see extensions
available


kot.append("name")


kot += ["please"]


kot.count


kot.capacity
```

```
kot.insert("your", atIndex: 2) //indexes always start with zero

kot += ["stupid!"]

kot.removeLast()

kot

kot.removeAtIndex(4)

//////////////////////////////////
//The following relate to chapter questions
//////////////////////////////////

var result = kot + aStringArray


kot.removeAll()
kot

aNewIntArray.isEmpty

//aNewIntArray.popLast()

aNewIntArray.insert(-1, atIndex: 0)

aNewIntArray.popLast()

aNewIntArray
```

```
var number = (4,5)
print(number)


var list = Array<Int>(count: 4, repeatedValue: 6)
var list2 = [Int](count: 5, repeatedValue: 7)

var myArray=[1,2,3,5,7,11,13,17]
```

Understanding Swift

```
import Cocoa

var str = "Hello, playground"

var pennies = 5
let enoughToBuyCandy = 5
if pennies >= enoughToBuyCandy{

    print("We may buy candy!")
}

var numberOfPenniesString = "pennies"

pennies = 4

if enoughToBuyCandy - pennies == 1{

    numberOfPenniesString = "penny"
}

if pennies >= enoughToBuyCandy{

    print("We can may candy!")

} else {

    print("We go home candy less \(enoughToBuyCandy - pennies) \(numberOfPenniesString)
short.")

}
```

```
pennies = 7

if enoughToBuyCandy - pennies == 1{

    numberOfPenniesString = "penny"
}

if pennies == enoughToBuyCandy{

    print("We may buy candy!")

} else if pennies > enoughToBuyCandy {

    print("We may get \( pennies - enoughToBuyCandy) pennies worth more of candy.")

}else{

    print("We go home candy less \(enoughToBuyCandy - pennies) \(numberOfPenniesString)
    short.")
}
```

```
//: Chapter 9 Playground - noun: a place where people can play

import Cocoa

var str = "Hello, playground"

var lemons = Int?()
var limes = Int!()

var peaches = 5
lemons = 5
limes = 5
lemons = nil
limes = nil
//peaches = nil //uncomment to see error

var apples = Int?()  //note this used to not have the () at the end but that has been changed.

if apples >= 1{

    print("We have \(apples)")

} else {  //this covers all else including nil

    print("We ain't got no apples today!")

}

let applesPerCrate = 20

//var appleCratesNeeded = apples/applesPerCrate //uncomment to see error and suggested
correction.
```

```
var potatoes = 1

var motatoes = Double(1)

var oranges = Int!()

let orangesPerCrate = 20

var pennies = 21

if pennies >= 100 {

    oranges = 5
}

var today = "Tuesday"

var plums = Int?()

if today == "Tuesday" {

    plums = 8
}

var plumsPerDay = plums! * 1  //the ! is necessary


var cuties = Int!() //(Clementie Oranges my duck loves them) note this used to not have the ()
at the end but that has been changed.
```

```swift
var numberOfCuties = cuties ?? 0  //Here we set  numberOfCuties to cuties if cuties is not nil
and 0 if cuties is equal to nil.

print(numberOfCuties)

if numberOfCuties >= 1{

    print("We have \(cuties)")

} else {

    print("We ain't got no cuties today!")

}

//We can also do it this way with an if else.

if cuties != nil {


    print("We have \(cuties)")

} else {

    print("We ain't got no cuties today!")

}

var bananas = Int?() //Explicitly an Int but this will not force unwrapped.

bananas = Int(arc4random_uniform(12)+1) //sets bananas to a random number. between
one and twelve
```

```
print("We have \(bananas!) bananas that is \((Double(bananas!)/12.00*100.0))% of a dozen")
```

//: Chapter 10 Playground - noun: a place where people can play

import Cocoa

var str = "Hello, playground"

```swift
for var i = 4.0; i < 7; i++ {
    print(i)
    print("i == \(i) \n")
}

var x:double_t = 0
for( x = 0; x < 4; x++){
    print(x)
}

for i in 4 ..< 7 {   //This uses the half-open range operator ..<
    for j in 7...10 {   //This uses the closed range operator ...
        print("\(i) \(j)")
    }
}

var myLoopArray = ["My","very", "eager","mother","just","served","up","nine","pies"]

var y = 0  //implicitly defined as Int

for( y = 0; y < 4; y++){
    print("myLoopArray[\(y)] == \(myLoopArray[y])")
}

myLoopArray.count
```

```
for( y = 0; y < myLoopArray.count; y++) {

    print("myLoopArray[\(y)] == \(myLoopArray[y])")

}


for planet in myLoopArray.enumerate() {


    print(planet)

}


for planet in myLoopArray {


    print(planet)

}



////////////////////////
// Questions
////////////////////////


for indice in 4...7 {


    print(myLoopArray[indice])

}
```

Understanding Swift

```
import Cocoa

var str = "Hello, playground"

var x = 6

while( x > -1){  //Asserts a condition to be met

  if( x != 0) {
    print("We are \(x) minutes from abreakthrough"); //does something we need done.\
  }else {

    print("We are having a abreakthrough");
  }

  x--; //gives us a way to exit the loop.
}


while x < 6 {

  print("We are on the verge of a breakthrough\(x)")
  x++
}
//and

x = 100

repeat { // repeat is now used instead of do in SWIFT
```

```
print("We are on the verge of a breakthrough\(x)")

  x += 100


}while x < 8 //we need to make sure the while loop ends at some time.
```

Understanding Swift

```swift
import Cocoa

var str = "Hello, playground"
```

//This is slightly different than the C and C++ version. Since break is not needed running answers together is different.

```swift
var dog = 5;

switch(dog)
{

case 0:
    print("Boxer");
    //breaks are not necessary
case 2:
    print("Irish Setter");

case 3:
    print("Doberman");

case 4:
    print("Springer Spaniel");

case 5,6:  //run together items are handled this way
    print("Unknown ");

default:
    print("Mutt");
}
```

```
print("\n\n");



var trueOrFalse = true

switch(trueOrFalse){

case true:

   print("true")

case false:

   print("false")

}
```

```
//: Chapter 13 Playground - noun: a place where people can play

import Cocoa

var str = "Hello, playground"

enum Numbers {  //Note word case before each value. This can be done differently but
without case you cannot have a rawValue—a value of some consistent type.

    case ZERO
    case ONE
    case TWO
    case THREE
    case FOUR
    case FIVE
    case SIX
    case SEVEN
    case EIGHT
    case NINE
    case TEN

}   //no need for a ;

//var count: enum Numbers = .EIGHT  //will give you a ERROR

var count1: Numbers = .EIGHT //will work.

//an implicit cast will also work.

var count = Numbers.EIGHT
```

```swift
enum PlantsNameHint {

    case my, very, eager
    case mother, just, served, up
    case nine, pies

}

var aPlanet = PlantsNameHint.served

switch(aPlanet){

case .my:

    print( "Mercury" )

case .very:

    print( "Venus" )

case .eager:

    print( "Earth" )

case .mother:

    print( "Mars" )

case .just:

    print( "Jupiter" )
```

```swift
case .served:

    print( "Saturn" )

case .up:

    print( "Uranus" )

case .nine:

    print( "Neptune" )

case .pies:

    print( "Poor Pluto" )


}

//I've added an x below to Numbers (xNumbers) to avoid a duplicate name error

enum xNumbers:Int {  //Note word case before each value.

    case ZERO
    case ONE
    case TWO
    case THREE
    case FOUR
    case FIVE
    case SIX
    case SEVEN
    case EIGHT
```

```
    case NINE
    case TEN

}   //no need for a ;

var time:xNumbers = .FIVE

if time == .FIVE {

    print(time.rawValue)


    let theTime = time.rawValue
    print(theTime)
    print(theTime)
}

enum YourInt: Int {

    case a,b,c

}

//works the same as with only the name of the enum different.

enum MyInt: Int {
    case a
    case b
    case c

}
```

```
//You do need to use the word case at least once to get rawValue.

/*
//Gives an error as the word case is missing
enum errorNum {

    a, b, c

}
*/


var myBubble = MyInt.c
var yourBubble = YourInt.c

print( myBubble.rawValue)
print( yourBubble.rawValue)

myBubble = MyInt( rawValue: 0)!

print(myBubble)

print(myBubble.rawValue)

var myNewBubble = MyInt(rawValue: 3)

//myNewBubble!.rawValue //here will cause an error!


myNewBubble = .b   // you will see b in your gutter.


enum MyInt2: Int {
```

```
    case a, b, c

}

var myNextNewBubble = MyInt2(rawValue:33)  //33 is way off, MyInt2 only has a 0, a 1 and
a 2.
myNextNewBubble = .a
myNextNewBubble!.rawValue

var myEvenNewerBubble = MyInt2.c
myEvenNewerBubble = MyInt2(rawValue:0)! //try removing the ! here and see the error
myEvenNewerBubble.rawValue
print (myEvenNewerBubble)

enum MyStringEnum: String {

    case sweet = "Sweet", young, thing

}

var string1 = MyStringEnum.sweet

string1.rawValue

string1 = .young

string1.rawValue



enum myCountingString: String {
```

```
    case one, two, three

}


var countTwo = myCountingString.two.rawValue


enum MyIntToo: Int{

    case a, b, c, d
}

let ace = MyIntToo.a

let doc = MyIntToo.a.rawValue

let myNewMyIntTooValue = ace.rawValue

//let myNewMyIntTooValue2 = doc.rawValue //uncomment to see error

//ace = .b  //uncomment to see a fixable error.




let diamonds = 5

//diamonds = 7 //uncomment to see error
```

This means remove the first two // on the line

diamonds = 7 // uncomment to see error

Understanding Swift

//: Chapter 14 Playground - noun: a place where people can play

import Cocoa

var aThousandIntArray = [Int](count: 1000, repeatedValue: 0)

let Mom = 4 // an inexplicitly created Int

var myExampleDictionary: [String : String] = ["Key" : "Value"]

var myDictionary:[String : String] = ["LastNameOne":"David", "LastNameTwo": "Lee", "LastNameThree":"Pat", "LastNameFour":"Sean"]

let Pap = ["Dad" , 7]

print(Pap)

for (surname, familyName) in myDictionary {

    print("\(surname) \(familyName)")

}

var myDictionary2: Dictionary<String , String> = ["LastNameOne":"David", "LastNameTwo": "Lee", "LastNameThree":"Pat", "LastNameFour":"Sean"]

```swift
var myDictionary3 = ["LastNameOne":"David", "LastNameTwo": "Lee",
"LastNameThree":"Pat", "LastNameFour":"Sean"]


var myFunFile = ["Dave": 11,"Pat" :12, "Sean" : 14.01]


for (key, value) in myFunFile{


   print("\(value * 0.202)")


}
let myNameNumber = myFunFile["Pat"]


//Will give us the value associated with ["Pat"] which is 12.


print( myNameNumber! * 0.202)  //We need the ! as myNameNumber is an optional


//var myNameNumber = myDictionary2["LastNameOne"]?[1] as? String



var myDictionaryTenTen:[Int : Int] = [ 0 : 5, 1 : 7, 2 : 9]


for var i = 3; i < 100; i++ {


   myDictionaryTenTen[i] = (i + (i % 10) * 2) + 5


}


print( myDictionaryTenTen)


var myresulting = myDictionaryTenTen[99]
myDictionaryTenTen[9]
```

myDictionaryTenTen.updateValue(33, forKey: 9)

myDictionaryTenTen[9]

myDictionaryTenTen.updateValue(32, forKey: 0)

myDictionaryTenTen[199] = (199 + (199 % 10) * 2) + 5

myDictionaryTenTen.count

myDictionaryTenTen[099] = (099 + (099 % 10) * 2) + 5

myDictionaryTenTen.count

myDictionaryTenTen[3*33] = (3*33 + (3*33 % 10) * 2) + 5

myDictionaryTenTen.count

myDictionaryTenTen[100]

myDictionaryTenTen[199]

myDictionaryTenTen.count

myDictionaryTenTen.removeValueForKey(199)

myDictionaryTenTen[199]

myDictionaryTenTen.count

myDictionaryTenTen[199] = 1000

```swift
for( whoCaresWhatICallTheKey, whoCaresWhatICallTheValue) in myDictionaryTenTen {

    print( "\(whoCaresWhatICallTheKey):\(whoCaresWhatICallTheValue)")
}

print(myDictionaryTenTen.keys)
print(myDictionaryTenTen.values)

for SomeSillyValue in myDictionaryTenTen.values {

    if SomeSillyValue % 11 == 0 {

        print("\(SomeSillyValue)")
    }
}
```

Understanding Swift

```
//: Chapter 15 Playground - noun: a place where people can play

import Cocoa


var str = "Hello, playground"

var aLetter = "o";

var anotherLetter: Character = "k"

//var word = aLetter + anotherLetter //uncomment to see error

var myWord1 = "n" //a String not a Character

var myWord2 = "o" //a String not a Character

var myFinalWord = myWord1 + myWord2  //this adds two Strings


//var aThirdLetter: Character = str[0] //crashes uncomment to see error


var i = 0

for myCharacter in str.characters{
    print (myCharacter)
}

for index in str.characters.indices {

    print("\(str[index])")
```

```
}
```

```
var myCharacter: [Character] = ["D","A","V","E"]
var myOtherCharacter = ["D,A,V,E"] //declares an array of Strings with one String so far.  and
gives us:


myOtherCharacter[0]  //proof that this is a one String array of Strings.


var myString: String = String(myCharacter) //joins an Array of Characters into a string


print(myString)



//myString.append("?") //uncomment to see error append adds Characters only


var myQuestionMark: Character = "?"
myString.append(myQuestionMark)


//var newWord = myString + myQuestionMark  //fails uncomment to see error


//var newWord1 = myString += myQuestionMark // fails uncomment to see error


var myString2: String = String(myCharacter) //Command click on String here to see
possiblities for String.



myString.startIndex  //we get 0 in the gutter. But that 0 is not readily available as an ordinary
int with value 0.
```

myString.**characters.count** //and we get 4 so No the "\n" is not included in the count. And since the index starts at 0 the "\n" is at position 4.

myString.**endIndex** //gives us 5. Which is the same as
myString.**characters.count**

myString.**endIndex.predecessor()** //this provides us with what we'd expect the last occupied index of the String

myString[myString.**endIndex.predecessor()**]

myString.**endIndex.predecessor().predecessor()**

myString[myString.**endIndex.predecessor()**] //this however gives us the Character at the predecessor() position that is the index before endIndex.

myString[myString.**endIndex.predecessor().predecessor()**] //takes us two steps back and gives us an "E."

myString.**characters.count**

myString[myString.**endIndex.predecessor().predecessor().predecessor().predecessor().predec essor()**]

myString.**startIndex.successor()**

myString.**startIndex.successor().successor()**

```
myString[myString.startIndex.successor()]

myString[myString.startIndex.successor().successor()]  //gives us "V"

myString.startIndex.successor() //works much like .predecessor except successor() moves
forward.

myString.endIndex.predecessor().successor()


for index in str.characters.indices {

    print("\(str[index])")

}


myString.startIndex.advancedBy(2)

myString[myString.startIndex.advancedBy(2)]

myString[myString.startIndex.advancedBy(4)]

var counter = 0  //counter must be set to an int not an index

while counter < str.characters.count {  // str.characters.count does return an Int.

    print(str[str.startIndex.advancedBy(counter)])  //advanced by takes the Int argument.

    counter++
}
```

myString.insert("!", atIndex: myString.endIndex) //doesn't overwrite but inserts at the endIndex of the string.

myString.removeAtIndex(myString.endIndex.predecessor().predecessor()) //removes the "?" we pushed forward.

print(myString)

var **countOfCharacters** = str.characters.count // str.characters.count returns an int

str.endIndex //remember we can't use this it is an index not an int.

var **counterNeg** = countOfCharacters

str.endIndex.advancedBy(-counterNeg)

while counterNeg > 0 {

   print(str[str.endIndex.advancedBy(-counterNeg)])
   counterNeg--
}

myString.insert("!", atIndex: myString.endIndex) //doesn't overwrite but inserts at the endIndex of the string.

```
myString.endIndex.predecessor()


myString.removeAtIndex(myString.endIndex.predecessor().predecessor()) //removes the "?"
we pushed forward.

print(myString)

print( "myString has \(myString.characters.count) characters.")

var aRange = str.startIndex.advancedBy(7)...str.startIndex.advancedBy(10)

//lets add some needed punctuation.

str.insert(".", atIndex: str.endIndex)

//What did the parachutist whose chute did not open say?

str.removeRange(aRange)
```

```
//: Chapter 16 Playground - noun: a place where people can play

import Cocoa

var str = "Hello, playground"


var myFavoriteFlag = "My favorite flag is "

myFavoriteFlag += "\u{2620}"

print(myFavoriteFlag)

var myString = "PROGRAMMER"

myString.hasPrefix("PR")  //gives true  this is the prefix
myString.hasSuffix("OG") //gives false  this is not the suffix
myString.hasSuffix("ER") //gives true   this is the suffix.

print( "myString has \(myString.characters.count) characters.")

//gives us "myString has 10 characters.\n"

myString.isEmpty //will give us false as there are characters there.

var aBlankString = ""  //set this to a blank string

var anotherBlankSting = String() //set this to a blank string

aBlankString.isEmpty    //gives us true
anotherBlankSting.isEmpty //gives us true
```

```
aBlankString = myString

if( aBlankString == myString){

    print("These two Strings are equal")

} else {

    print("\u{2620}")

}
```

Understanding Swift

```
import Cocoa

var str = "Hello, playground"

struct businessCard {

    var firstName = String?()
    var middleName = String?()
    var surName = String?()
    var age = Int?()
    var isFemale = Bool?()

}


//another way to do it would be to make the age 0 for unfinished cards.  Although var age = 0
above would be simpler.

var myCard = businessCard(firstName: nil, middleName: nil, surName: nil, age: 0, isFemale:
nil)

//Phone numbers could be an Int or a String.  Lets just use an Int here.

var myBusinessCardDictionary:[Int : businessCard] = [0:myCard]

//we can print individual values this way
print(myCard.age)

//Lets make a dictionary
```

```
//to put a phone number in we actually have to remove the key identified by 0

myBusinessCardDictionary.removeValueForKey(0)

//now our dictionary is empty
//print(myBusinessCardDictionary)

//lets add values to our myCard

//We will use a phone number for the key

myBusinessCardDictionary = [5555551212:myCard]


//we can fill in our blank card

if myCard.age == 0 {

    myCard.firstName = "Bob"
    myCard.middleName = "David"
    myCard.surName = "Cats"
    myCard.age = 33
    myCard.isFemale = false

}

//then we can update the value myCard
myBusinessCardDictionary.updateValue(myCard, forKey: 5555551212)


var myCard2 = businessCard(firstName: "Jan", middleName: "Michelle", surName: "Dogs",
age: 32, isFemale: true)
```

```
myBusinessCardDictionary[5555551020] = myCard2

//print(myBusinessCardDictionary)

func upDateMyCardAge( myCard: businessCard, NewValueForAge: Int)->businessCard{

    var newAgeCard = myCard

    newAgeCard.age = NewValueForAge


    return newAgeCard
}

myBusinessCardDictionary.updateValue(upDateMyCardAge( myCard, NewValueForAge:
27), forKey: 5555551020)


print(myBusinessCardDictionary)
```

```
//: Chapter 18 Playground - noun: a place where people can play

import Cocoa

var str = "Hello, playground"

//: Playground - noun: a place where people can play

import Cocoa



var listOfNumbers = [11,14,56,61,4,2]

func giveMeTheAverageMileage(listOfNumbers: Array<Int>) -> Int{

var total = 0

for var i = 0; i < listOfNumbers.count; i++ {  //we don't need to know how many items
                                     //our array has Swift takes care of that for
us.

total += listOfNumbers[i]
}


return total

}

print(giveMeTheAverageMileage(listOfNumbers))
```

Understanding Swift

```
//Here is my function taking a string and returning a prefix of length.

func returnPrefix(wordToPrefix:String, lengthOfPrefixToReturn: Int) ->String  {


    //check to make sure the length to return is greater than 0

    if lengthOfPrefixToReturn == 0 {

        return ""
    }
    //create a counter of type Int (implicitly)

    var nextIndexMarker = 1


    //set up an array of Characters and initialize it with the first Character in our string

    var aPrefix:[Character] = [wordToPrefix[wordToPrefix.startIndex]]

    //the three lines below are only here to show you their values before using them
    lengthOfPrefixToReturn
    nextIndexMarker
    wordToPrefix.characters.count


    //we'll use a while loop to add to the Character Array
    while nextIndexMarker < wordToPrefix.characters.count && lengthOfPrefixToReturn >
nextIndexMarker {


aPrefix.append(wordToPrefix[wordToPrefix.startIndex.advancedBy(nextIndexMarker)])
```

```
    nextIndexMarker++
  }


  // As show previously we can convert an array of Characters into a Sting with String()
  //the :String below isn't really necessary

  let result:String = String(aPrefix)

  //as in C and C++ we must furnish a return value
  return(result)

}

//call the function
var myPrefixString = returnPrefix(str,lengthOfPrefixToReturn: 3)

//print our result

print(myPrefixString)


///////////////////////
/// making an update card age function
///////////////////////


//we need to restate a few things from Chapter 17

struct businessCard {

  var firstName = String?()
```

```
    var middleName = String?()
    var surName = String?()
    var age = Int?()
    var isFemale = Bool?()


}


var myCard = businessCard(firstName: "Tom", middleName: "NMN", surName: "Swift", age:
14, isFemale: false)


var myBusinessCardDictionary:[Int : businessCard]


myBusinessCardDictionary = [5555551212:myCard]



func upDateMyCardAge( myCard: businessCard, NewValueForAge: Int)->businessCard{


    var newAgeCard =  myCard


    newAgeCard.age =  NewValueForAge



    return newAgeCard
}


myBusinessCardDictionary.updateValue(upDateMyCardAge( myCard, NewValueForAge:
27), forKey: 5555551212)


//print(myBusinessCardDictionary[0]) //uncomment to see error


print(myBusinessCardDictionary[5555551212])
```

```
func SOMEFUNC(anIntValue:Int)->Int{

    return(anIntValue)  //returning the value entered should always be exhaustive.
}

var valueToSwitchOn =  5

switch(valueToSwitchOn){

case 1:

   print("Opps")

case 2:

   print("Whoops")

case SOMEFUNC(valueToSwitchOn):

   print("Success if Swift doesn't ask for a default.")

default: //comment out both this and line below to see what happens

    print("This will never print") //comment this out too

}
```

```
//
//  main.cpp
//  pointerCrashExampleForConditionals
//
//  Created by David Curran on 1/9/16.
//  Copyright © 2016 David Francis Curran. All rights reserved.
//

#include <iostream>
using namespace std;

int main(int argc, const char * argv[]) {



    //You can paste this entire section into a console project set up for C++

    int book = 1999334;  //we have put a book # 1999334 on the shelf.

    int *cardForBookYetToBeEntered = 0;

    cout << "cardForBookYetToBeEntered = " << cardForBookYetToBeEntered << " a blank
card. \n\n";

    int *libraryCardPtr = &book; //This  is our library reference card pointing to our book.
&book is the shelf location of book


    cout << "*libraryCardPtr is: " << *libraryCardPtr << " the book itself.\nlibraryCardPtr == "
<< libraryCardPtr << " is the books location in memory. \nand book == " << book << " the
book itself same as *libraryCardPtr\n\n"; // value pointed to by pointer
```

libraryCardPtr = 0; //we set the library card to blank

cout << "Now we will set libraryCardPtr to zero. libraryCardPtr = " << libraryCardPtr << "\n\n";

cout << "Because libraryCardPtr is Null referencing *libraryCardPtr would cause a crash and so cannot be referenced. \n libraryCardPtr == " << libraryCardPtr << "\nand book == " << book << " it is still on the shelf but is no longer pointed to by the card. The card is blank. \n\n"; // value pointed to by pointer

cout << "We get an ERROR if we try to locate the book via the card as the card libraryCardPtr = " <<libraryCardPtr << " \n\n";

//The other way to cause an ERROR is when we delete the book rather than the card.

int size = 1;

int *intBlockPtr = (int*)malloc(size*sizeof(int));

cout << *intBlockPtr << " = intBlockPtr\n\n";

*intBlockPtr += 10000789; //we have created shelf space and added book 10000789

cout << "*intBlockPtr == " << *intBlockPtr << "\n\n";

cout << "intBlockPtr == " << intBlockPtr << "\n\n";

cout << "Now we free(intBlockPt\n\n"; //we have deleted the shelves and floor

free(intBlockPtr);

```
    cout << " intBlockPtr = "<< intBlockPtr << "\n\n";  //  the pointer still points at the
location which is not there

    cout << *intBlockPtr << " = intBlockPtr\n\n";

    return 0;
}
```

```
//
//  main.c
//  Chapter12Switches
//
//  Created by David Curran on 1/9/16.
//  Copyright © 2016 David Francis Curran. All rights reserved.
//


#include <stdio.h>

int main(int argc, const char * argv[]) {



    int dog = 5;

    switch(dog)
    {
        case 0:
            printf("Boxer");
            break;  //breaks are necessary after each unless you want to run them together
        case 2:
            printf("Irish Setter");
            break;
        case 3:
            printf("Doberman");
            break;
        case 4:
            printf("Springer Spaniel");
            break;
        case 5:
            printf("Unknown "); //no break and these combine
```

```
    default:
        printf("Mutt");
    }
    printf("\n\n");


    return 0;
}
```

```
//
//  main.swift
//  ChapterTwelveSwitchSwift
//
//  Created by David Curran on 1/9/16.
//  Copyright © 2016 David Francis Curran. All rights reserved.
//

import Foundation

print("Hello, World!")//
//  main.swift
//  switchByEnteredString
//
//  Created by David Curran on 12/8/15.
//  Copyright © 2015 David Francis Curran. All rights reserved.
//

import Foundation

func userEnteredData() -> String{

    let userTypedIn = NSFileHandle.fileHandleWithStandardInput()

    let myEnteredString = userTypedIn.availableData

    return NSString(data: myEnteredString, encoding:NSUTF8StringEncoding) as! String
}
print( "Please enter your gender")

var reply = String!()
```

```
reply = userEnteredData()

var replyForSwitch  = reply ?? "Error "  //nil coalescing operator to prevent an error.



switch(replyForSwitch){

case "Error":

    print("There has been a ERROR please try again!")


 //this is the corrected case below

case "Male\n","M\n","MALE\n","m\n","male\n":

    print( "Thank you sir!")
default:  //if you are not male…
    print( "Thank you ma'am'!")


}
```

```c
//
//  main.c
//  EnumTests
//
//  Created by David Curran on 1/9/15.
//  Copyright © 2015 David Francis Curran. All rights reserved.
//

#include <stdio.h>

int main(int argc, const char * argv[]) {


    enum Numbers {

        ZERO, ONE, TWO, THREE, FOUR, FIVE, SIX, SEVEN, EIGHT, NINE, TEN

    };


    enum Numbers nowTime = THREE;

    printf("\nnowTime is == %d and THREE is == %d\n", nowTime,THREE);

    nowTime = TEN;

    printf("\nnowTime is == %d and TEN is == %d\n", nowTime,TEN);

    nowTime = 15;

    printf("\nnowTime is == %d and 15 is == %d\n", nowTime,15);
```

```
    return 0;
}
```

```
//
//  main.c
//  Chapter15.7PastEndInC
//
//  Created by David Curran on 1/10/16.
//  Copyright © 2016 David Francis Curran. All rights reserved.
//

#include <stdio.h>

int main(int argc, const char * argv[]) {

    char name[] = "Dave";
    printf("%c\n", name[5]);


    return 0;
}
```

```cpp
//
//  main.cpp
//  Chapter18FunctionExample
//
//  Created by David Curran on 1/10/16.
//  Copyright © 2016 David Francis Curran. All rights reserved.
//

#include <iostream>
using namespace std;


int giveMeTheAverageMileage( int myMileArray[], int entriesTotal){

    int result = 0;

    for( int x = 0; x < entriesTotal; x++ ){

        result += myMileArray[x];
    }
    return result;
}

int doIt( int forbar[], int foo){

    int w = 0;

    for( int x = 0; x < foo; x++ ){

        w += forbar[x];
    }
```

```
    return w;
}


int main(int argc, const char * argv[]) {



    int distance[6] = {11,14,56,61,4,2};

    cout << "Average milage == " << giveMeTheAverageMileage(distance, 6) << "\n\n";
    cout << "Average milage is also == " << doIt(distance, 6) << "\n\n";

    return 0;
}
```

www.ingramcontent.com/pod-product-compliance
Lightning Source LLC
Chambersburg PA
CBHW071109050326
40690CB00008B/1162